Lindsay Llady

The Apostle of the Ardennes

Lindsay Llady

The Apostle of the Ardennes

ISBN/EAN: 9783741156090

Manufactured in Europe, USA, Canada, Australia, Japa

Cover: Foto ©Lupo / pixelio.de

Manufactured and distributed by brebook publishing software (www.brebook.com)

Lindsay Llady

The Apostle of the Ardennes

I

"The prince will hunt to-morrow," ran the word,
Pass'd on, as in some village game a ring
Is slipt from touch to touch.

        "His grace will hunt."

"Yea, but to-morrow?"

        " Ay, just as to-day."

And through the castle hall, down winding stairs,
Out by the courtyard, and beyond the gate,
That echo, "yea, to-morrow," flitted on,
Like to a spectre, scattering nameless fear.

THE APOSTLE OF THE ARDENNES

O godless ruler! might he not forego
For one scant solemn day within the year—
The solemnest of all our Christian year—
His boisterous raid of hunting, with its greed
Of creatures' pulse, its lust of butchery
Wove into pageant, regally decked out—
Earth's wanton holocaust spread out ablaze
To hide the angels' sorrowful pale brows?
Not one short morn, nay, not that clouded hour
When Christ for us hung on the shameful rood,
A stainless sacrifice for our dark deeds?
What! This fierce hunter—Esau among men—
Would so forsake fast, vigil, penance, prayer,
And all the genuflexions of the just,
And all the sorrowed sighings of the meek,
To plunder forests wild and isolate
Where leaves bud tremulous green, to scare and slay
The peaceful inmates in their deep retreat,
To sully tepid winds with bugle blare,
Trampling the virgin sward with horses' hoofs,

THE APOSTLE OF THE ARDENNES

Scarring pure grass with slaughtered innocence,
Reddening the bushes by rough hurtful hands
And tracks of murderous desolating pain—
On such a day, O Christ, on such a day!

Thus sped that saying fleetly through the gate,
Unchallenged by the watch, adown the steep,
Past track of brushwood and pale bursting thorn,
And rugged crags where ivy garlands clung
Or holly bushes crowded, and dusk yew
Made here and there a blot that showed the rest
More golden in the flickering afternoon.

Deep down, the hamlet lay amid green fields,
Crouched by the castle's fastness as a kid,
Half tame, half wild, lies at the goat-herd's feet,
Knowing there's safety. But, across the plain,
Drawn as a silver braid to mark the page
Of some great tome, a little river wound,
Skirting the mystic darkness of the forest

THE APOSTLE OF THE ARDENNES

That loomed, a heavy cloud, from east to west,
Horizon on horizon of tree-tops,
Swelling to curve or straightening into line,
Far as keen eye might peer, grown well-nigh blue
Where blueness of the sky dipped down to it,
Mirrored as in the sea. And few folks knew
What lay within, or what beyond, so vast
And weird and fearsome was that wooded realm:
The Ardennes forest of wide-world renown.

Now, under eaves and beams of such poor huts
As made the village, paused the sullen speech,
To linger stagnant in the mind of boors.

"To-morrow; ay, Good Friday."

"Dare he hunt?
The prince?"

"Yea, so. Forsooth! Laws are not framed

THE APOSTLE OF THE ARDENNES

For noble knights or royal kith and kin.
Not e'en God's laws. Ne'er knew he but one way,
His own, through mire of cruelty and blood.
Whom should he heed? He does not toil or sweat,
As common hinds must toil for roof and bread,
To lift their children from the gutter's filth,
And earn an ell or two of cloth of frieze.
Why should he fast that has good cheer to hand?
Why kneel on stone that can in velvet ride,
And at free will build laws and gibbets both?"
So spake some froward spirits of the place,
In rancorous underbreath, yet quick abashed,
For all were serfs, their heads press'd down by yoke
Of fear and need. Thus cattle learn to stand,
Patient, dull-eyed, and dumb, that drag the cart.

High in the castle yard, tongues wagged at ease.
There loitered serving men, adepts to prate,
And stable boys and kitchen wenches too,
And armourers, hurrying past the tilting-ground

THE APOSTLE OF THE ARDENNES

From out a shed where blazed the heated forge
In red fierce shafts that leaped awhile, and fell,
And lit dismembered harness hung about:
Head-pieces, breast-plates, gauntlets, closely heaped
By lance or axe, gleaming through open doors.
While, two and two, boy pages strolled along,
Arm within arm, a-chattering as they came,
With many an ominous grave shake of head
As doomed the whole world. Next, the prince's squire,
To hear the cause of all this malcontent;
And men-at-arms, in groups and knots, stood by,
Well pleased that any strife should taint the air.
(Of late their barracks were too peaceful far.)

"Prithee, who'll bell the cat? Our good Lord Hubert—
Who, when a lad, scarce out of leading strings,
A second David, tamed great Ebroin—
Is hot of temper and more swift of hand,
Being of southern stock, than an he were
Born of Louvain indeed. So may ye see

THE APOSTLE OF THE ARDENNES

Some Orient plant, late nurtured in our garth,
Which, at the beckoning of a July sun,
Will stretch and climb with giant shoot and stem,
Such as our land knew not.   Nor all past pruning
Of Pepin's court, nor grace nor gentleness
Of Louvain's daughter, yon too gracious spouse,
Can stay the fierce wrath of that alien mind,
(Now he be grown to unrestricted power,)
If but some irksome finger of advice
Kindle the angry blood of Aquitaine,
Ruffling his hunting tunic's fringe.   Heard you
How but last week our Abbot fann'd the flame
By solemn words of well-deserved reproof,
So was forbade the castle?   Then, who'll speak?"

"Not I."

   "Nor I."

      "On his own head his sin,
And let the powers of ill protect their own!"

THE APOSTLE OF THE ARDENNES

    Different the picture of the inner court.
A rounded mead of grass, by stone flags hemmed,
Spaced by smooth bays and oleander trees
That rose from wooden troughs, a pleasaunce made,
Where flickered sunny specks 'mid shadows deep,
And sapphire-throated peacocks stalked in pride
To seize the bread doled out by dainty hands
Of one who leaned from casement ledge above.

A narrow stair of marble climbed to lead
Straight to the lady's bower, and on the steps
Sat girl Sabrina, dark-eyed, mischievous,
Favourite 'mong maids of honour, while her laugh
Low rippled as for joyance of itself,
Evoked by greed of those resplendent birds
That snapped and choked and guzzled at her feet.

But she who sat yet loftier, leaning out—
Her white arm laden with broad bands of gold,
Her rich-ringed fingers filled with broken bread—

THE APOSTLE OF THE ARDENNES

Was that princess, named Floriban the Fair,
Sweet second self to Hubert—she, with face
Rose-pink, whose kind grey eyes most innocent,
Shining as do some sky-lit water-pools
Nigh to the fringe of forests windy blown,
Gleamed under cloudy waving wreaths of hair
Perplexing in its many-tinted shades,
Here brown, there gold, next dusky, well-nigh red,
Close plaited right and left with turquoise knots,
And 'gainst the grey stone arch all luminous.

She likewise laughed, for sunny were her moods;
Thoughtless she was, and young, in love with life.
Had life not greeted her with joys and gems,
And peace and plenty—Care and Grief chained up,
As hounds may be that do not dare to bay
From some dark unsought kennel out of sight?

She starts, she turns. A footstep on the floor
Has echoed in her ear and in her heart,

THE APOSTLE OF THE ARDENNES

While out fond eyes the love-light softly peers
To meet a welcome kiss from him whose hand
Garlands her neck.

           " My lord, what sport?"

                          "Good, good.
The thicket, sparsely touched with emerald, roofed
Our hot eyes from the sun, and o'er the ground
Our joyous steeds, swift arrows in the wind,
Sped bravely. Faith! my heart throbs high once more,
Repeating such gay tune it sang this morn,
When thought that daring hunt recalls. The hounds,
Eager as we, lowly their voices pitched
As ours, and thrilled with like expectancy,
Yet soon were off in full and baying cry.
And then—ah! 'twas a luckless counterstroke
Fate dealt yon hapless varlet, Rolf the Red!
A grim grey boar slipt through the maze of dogs,
Most dexterous, and with savage tusk ripped up

THE APOSTLE OF THE ARDENNES

The fellow's thigh—my cutlass brought him down—
I'd say the quadruped—a worthy foe,
Of noble race, huge, fiercely-natured—would
'Twere morn again, I'd gladly chase his double
Betwixt the netted tree-trunks of Ardennes!"

Slow down the marble stair Sabrina crept,
Hearing the prince, though without care of words.
Well witting that her mistress Floriban
Had now but meagre need of her, she dropt
Among the enquiring peacocks as a rose,
White-petalled and all fragrant, oft-time falls,
In storm of summer, on the tender sward—
Unhurt and silent. There a moment stayed;
Then, drawn to her slim height, sped swift away,
Skirting the dusky walls and buttressed nooks—
A shadow on the shadowy stony paths—
Singing beneath her breath the while she ran
A pretty rhyme wed to an ancient tune,
Right fanciful, that snared her wandering thought.

THE APOSTLE OF THE ARDENNES

"Is it joy, or is it grief,
When Love holds my heart in fief?

Joy is close akin to pain;
Scarce might any count the gain.

Pain is near akin to pleasure—
Who would stay to weigh the measure?"

Then presently, beyond the court, she took
A few short steps into the noisy yard,
(For maids are lured by sound as moths by light,)
And so, beside the gate-house, joined the crowd,
The chattering, laughing, wrangling, motley crowd.
O'er all, the mellow light of afternoon
Shed glamour, gilding lines of battlement,
Or crenelled roof, or here and there a clasp
Of silver in a page's cap, or curl
Strayed from beneath a serving-woman's coif,
Or brought some scarlet hose to strong relief,

THE APOSTLE OF THE ARDENNES

Or touched the foamy flank of chestnut steeds
That stood distressed, limp-kneed, with hanging heads,
Wearied by heavy labour of the chase,
Waiting their grooming when the turn should come
At hand of whistling lads with water cans.
And in the midst Red Rolf lay, sighing loud,
Prone on the ground just where he first was laid;
Astride of him the barber, plying tools
And tying cloths and dressing of the wound—
A kindly, scarce a grateful task, in truth.
So stood the crowd of household folk agape,
(Children are pleased if e'er a squall come by,
Bringing adventure and excitement new,)
The men contemptuous, smiling, as should say,
"Myself has known a greater hurt than this,"
The womankind a-tiptoe, herding close,
Eager yet shy, each holding hard her breath,
With neck outstretched. But she, Sabrina, drew
An arm's length back, shrinking from sight of pain,
Shivering for chill, as though dark omens pressed

THE APOSTLE OF THE ARDENNES

Across the golden sunshine of her path,
To soil the hem of her white trailing robe.

Then, strange and sudden, from some outer gate
Uprose a voice, and all eyes turned to look
Where, by the drawbridge, toward the bridle path,
Upon a knoll of rugged heathered ground,
A barefoot friar stood, with outstretched arm,
His cowl thrown back, his fervid eyes heav'n-raised,
His agèd face majestic in such wrath
As, like the knotted cord about his loins,
Might fain spell flagellation to the crowd,
Syllabling penance and dire punishment.

"Shame on ye, wantons! shame, accursèd loons!
Meet servants of a shameless impious lord.
Wot ye not how this day—of which ye reck
As little as of yonder offal heap
The swift-bill'd kites are cleansing—which ye spend
In worldly toil and cruel sensual chase,

THE APOSTLE OF THE ARDENNES

Heeding the thirsting cry of flesh-taught hounds
Beyond the bitter wailing of your souls—
This very day is by our great church named
Thursday the Holy, being the envoy sent
As harbinger, black-draped, and torch in hand,
Of that most sorrowing Friday when the world
Bows down in gloom through weeping for her Lord?
Shame on ye all! And shame the most to him
Who rules this house! For sure, unless he turn,
From velvet ways, to press anew life's path
Upon his knees, to feel the prick of thorns
Which holy saints have trodden for their joy,
Because that Christ such thorns wore on His brow;
Unless he bring with him your chastened hearts,
As pious gifts, to offer at God's shrine;
Unless he weep where he has laughed, and pray
Where he rough-rode, and cross and beat his breast,
And scourge the devils of profanity
From out his halls and gates—behold, I say,
They that are greater than mine humble self

THE APOSTLE OF THE ARDENNES

Shall rule him excommunicate.   Yea, Death,
A living death, far from all living springs
Of hope and piety, shall clog his days;
A strangling vulture on his entrails feed,
And force its talons through the festering years
That still cling close unto the bones of life.
Yea, worse hereafter!   Through the depths of hell
His spirit obstinate shall rot in flame,
And, mouldering, die not.   Was not Cain an out-
    cast?
E'en he, had he shared blessing of our church,
Turning aside from black temptation's road,
Haply had cleansed his soul.   But this fierce man—
This savage prince—that knows yet will not know,
So naught may plead of childlike ignorance,
He is a sinner more than sinful Cain.
Lawless, he daily, hourly, crucifies
Through his own sin the sinless Son of God;
While Cain slew in his haste a human brother,
Yet quailed before the curse."

THE APOSTLE OF THE ARDENNES

       The friar ceased
His vengeful strain, and sudden silence fell
Upon the awe-struck crowd.

       Till—as at eve
In summer may be seen, across some lake
Spellbound and stagnant through the burning day,
A ripple from the shadowy coast draw nigh,
Parting the water with a shuddering line,
That grows and lengthens o'er the mere of glass
Whose face is touched and quickened by a breath
Unfelt as yet in the still atmosphere—
There passed a quivering dread among the folk
That huddled closely, stunned, and much amazed,
Each having stayed his hand from work, and paused
Just where he stood, to hear the anathema
Of him who now fled swift away from sight,
Down to the rocky vale, with leap on leap,
Unscathed and unpursued. Then wenches wept
Big tears down pallid cheeks, but gave no sob,

THE APOSTLE OF THE ARDENNES

And muttered spells, deeming they'd seen a ghost.
Only the wounded man, who, in the midst
Lay unassisted and forgot, made moan—
None heeded him—till some, in staring trance,
Moved slow to tend him.

                    But Sabrina ran,
Her hands upon her ears, as though to oust
The friar's menace, should it jar again,
Sharp-toned, upon her brain, pursuing her
With echoed thunders from God's throne; so ran
To her lone turret, seeking safe retreat,
And, barring out all direful prophecies,
Calling on Freya, that she lend kind aid.

II

How the Lady Floriban grew sad with dire foreboding.

II

Among her maids sat Floriban the Fair.
Some at a loom wove tapestry, some span
Flax foam-waves into thread upon a wheel,
Some 'broidered seams of garments or of cloths;
And every now and then, as 'twere the path
Of summer wind-gusts through encloistered trees,
A lilting music strayed across the room,
For white hands struck a dulcimer or lute,
And twanged the moaning strings till beams and roof
Vibrated with a faint reluctant thrill,
Ebbing to stillness.

                Fairest fair, in truth,
Was Floriban.   On cushioned alabaster
She lay, her sweet face flushed, her eager ken

THE APOSTLE OF THE ARDENNES

Searching the landscape by her casement framed,
For something far to sight yet near to heart.
Yea, are not alway women's eyes so bent?
Yon forest made the girdle of her world.
There, in the distant valley, crossing fields,
And brooks, and copses, one small distant speck
(Which was her god) out-distanced kindred specks,
And shone, the lode-star of all hopefulness;
While at such simple vision her fond eyes
Brimmed o'er each moment with felicity—
Dew-laden blossoms, burdensome and wet
For very yearning.

"Look, Sabrina, look,
My lord rides foremost—oh, I mark him well!
He'll ever lead, ay, wheresoe'er he go,
Outrunning power and jealousy of kings,
As now he heads the huntsmen and the hounds.
Alas, but I'm aweary—sing, my girl,
Some joyous song to cheer this loneliness."

THE APOSTLE OF THE ARDENNES

"Ay, Madam, here's a ditty wrought for you.
The very woods and thickets teem of it,
The rushes breathe it by the silvered mere,
The throstle weaves such ballads, hawthorn buds
Unfold them on the boughs."

"Quick; sing, child, sing."

Then did Sabrina lay the needle by
Wherewith she pricked upon a canvas sheet,
In gaudy wools or touch of shining silk,
A semblance of fierce battle, combatants
Ruddy of cheek and wondrous swarth of eye,
Whose lengthy spears and giant battle-axes
Dealt grievous hurt alike to friends and foes.
So, clasping close her hands about her knees,
In dulcet tone she carolled merrily:

"Three king's daughters sat on the green.
(With a hey, my heart, and a hey derry down,)
They were the fairest that ever were seen—

THE APOSTLE OF THE ARDENNES

(With a hey, my heart, and a ho.)
  They sat and sang through the summer day,
  And two were sad, but the third was gay—
(With a hey, my heart, and a ho.)

  Three brave warriors came riding by,
(With a hey, my heart, and a hey derry down,)
  On their milk-white steeds they all drew nigh—
(With a hey, my heart, and a ho.)
  Then each he kneeled on the grassy floor,
  And two said much, but the third said more—
(With a hey, my heart, and a ho.)

  Six wild swans flew across the lea,
(With a hey, my heart, and a hey derry down,)
  Over the hills and beyond the sea—
(With a hey, my heart, and a ho.)
  And three brave steeds were left on the green,
  But the king's fair daughters were never more seen—
(With a hey, my heart, and a ho.)"

THE APOSTLE OF THE ARDENNES

" 'Tis passing pleasant," grave spake Floriban;
"Yet fairy-lore's but tinsel, while true gold
Is life, decked with the jewels of our earth:
Love, constancy, and truth—a matchless crown!
Sabrina, thou hast never known Love's call,
Wherefore thou may'st not frame his alphabet.
A lover sighs: Dear heart! and she, his queen,
Flies to his arms, as when delight of Spring
Glows on the earth in crocus-time; but next,
Coy minstrels to that first exultant kiss,
All words of love hang back. I cannot teach
    thee.
To tell such secret were to tear its robe
From off the idol of my sanctuary.
Content thee. If one night the changing moons
Bring to thee words one thousandth part as sweet,
As those which Hubert spake. . . . Nay, I've a
    heartache.
Some strange presentment binds my soul to-day
With cords and clinging shrouds of dull grey grief."

THE APOSTLE OF THE ARDENNES

Then cried Sabrina, springing from her seat:
" A chorus, girls! Throw toil aside, and sing!
Clap hands, tap feet, to mark the rhythm of time
That through your lilting should incessantly
Clang as the gallop of yon horses' hoofs,
Seeking th' unharboured chace, while huntsmen cry:
' *Now to him, to him, ay, that's he, that's he!*
That's he, good knave, look 'ware, 'ware, 'ware! Look 'ware!' "

At this the maidens, by her humour touched,
Laughed out, and, from the shuttle or the threads,
Let slim white fingers truant play awhile
To beat as 'twere with measured drums or gongs;
While far o'erhead the music floated clear,
And rose free-winged unto a gold-beamed roof,
Blending young voices—some more high, some low—
As separate strings of pearl are roped in one:

THE APOSTLE OF THE ARDENNES

"Forth from the forest,
Forth comes the west wind.
Hark how the branches
Murmur and quiver,
Quiver and whisper,
Deep in the forest!

Forth from the mountain,
Forth comes the tempest,
Rolling and raging,
Bringing the snow-drift,
Bringing the grey mist,
High from the mountain.

Down by the orchard,
Rides my belovèd,
Home from the battle,
Shining in armour,
Singing a love-song,
Gay by the orchard."

THE APOSTLE OF THE ARDENNES

But Floriban sat silent for a while,
As though she heard not, so 'twas deemed a sign
For courtier silence, and all tongues grew dumb.
There only prattled whirring busy wheels,
Or treadles; only clacked the click of pins.
Till presently the princess, beckoning
Sabrina, bade her crouch, and, with a hand
Soft nestling close to hers, spake fast and low,
So no strange ear should garner in the words,
That murmured forth their tremulous monotone,
Ceasing but seldom, being like hum of bees
Who stir yet scarcely settle 'mong the limes.

"Sabrina, hast thou never dreamed a dream
Which flares more glaring true than life itself,
Just as o'er-vivid storm-light in the sky
Dulls by its searing stroke our torches' gleam
Or lanthorns' glimmer? Late, late yesternight,
'Twas thus with me; this day seems but a dream,
Pulseless and vague and wan, the while that vision

THE APOSTLE OF THE ARDENNES

Throbs keen and white of heat, and burns my brain,
All else out-shutting—I'll not 'scape from it."

" Dear lady, hush! Blear phantoms such as these,
Will-o'-the-wisps, fade at Aurora's dawn,
Being counterfeits; the saffron-mantled goddess
Snuffs out such feeble ghosts; nay, sure, I've heard,
They track the steps of promised motherhood.
Soon, soon, princess, thy little one—for whom
Our hopes are morning-roseate—he'll be ours,
To laugh and prate with! Yea, our wish outstrips
Slow Time, so makes our fair dreams truth already.
Methinks, e'en now I hold the babe to kiss!"

" Nay, girl; I've prescience—and that's sorrowful.
We women own a strong-built second sight,
Because our form's so weakly. Hear my dream;
And haply thou, kind prop of lonely hours,
Shalt shudder with me for sweet company.

" Meseemed on this my couch I lay—stretched low,

THE APOSTLE OF THE ARDENNES

Limbs garmented of white, hair in long strands
Loose to the knees, with body wan and stiff,
And hands clasped meek on breast, where likewise lay
A frozen callow thing I'd ne'er yet seen,
A new-born voiceless babe, of marble wrought,
That breathed not, though my fingers touched its heart.
These eyes were pressed as though with leaden weight,
Yet through the lids I stared; yon doorway gaped,
The curtain thrown aside; and there, Sabrina,
Thou stood'st a-weeping, and thy tears dript down,
And trickled, as when on the castle roof
Slow-measured drops foretell a rushing storm.
Yet moved I not. The darkling doorway gaped,
And I looked—looked—a-wondering what beyond—
Till sudden rang a footfall by the stair—
A footfall that I knew albeit I dreamed—
And close it drew and close, anigh my bed,
So nigh, I tasted the rich pulsing life
Burst on my chillness—as the sun in May
Warms the dull earth—yet, yet, I might not move.

THE APOSTLE OF THE ARDENNES

But from my heart up crept a sullen pain,
Up to the lids of my poor prisoned eyes,
And sought the face of him who pressed anear;
Yea, as though anguish stood me 'stead of sight!
Thus was I 'ware he bent him down and kneeled;
Kneeled—he who ne'er has bowed to God or man—
Kneeled close beside us where so dead we lay,
His wife and child—his little child and wife!
And then—Sabrina, still it wrings my heart—
He wept! The tears struck on the silken ledge;
I heard the thud of each as 'twere a blow.
(When morning dawned I sought the stain of them.
No stain I found, albeit I bruised my lips
Where should have been the blur.) I say he prayed—
He who ne'er yet to Heaven has raised a hand,
Nor sped a shaft of prayer. Girl, dost thou hear?
He prayed—as might a reverent acolyte,
Gentle of voice, unwitting of the world,
Bearing a taper to the chancel steps—
He, Hubert, whom his thwarted knights in hall

THE APOSTLE OF THE ARDENNES

Oft liken to the wild boar or the wolf,
Whose untamed fierceness and most sumptuous
  pride
Give priests and kings alike a haughty gibe
For courtesy of welcome—he, whose voice
Wanes tender only when my twain fond arms
Wreathe vine-like round the column of his throat;
Whose eye dilates to keenness in the chase—
His haggard being more merciful—whose hand
Through deepest sleep oft gropes for lance or axe—
He prayed! And at the sight my tortured soul
Burst bonds of silence, and I shrieked and woke."

" Madam, in pity! See, for you this world
Grows thick with grace, as doth yon fertile plain,
Where April, from her shimmering veil of green,
Peeps shyly out at Phoebus. Scarce 'tis past
Your crocus-time of love, that but makes way
For lovelier daffadill, and hyacinth,
Which spread their perfumed carpet at your feet,

THE APOSTLE OF THE ARDENNES

Till later, still in summer of your days,
Roses shall bud and cluster—yea, believe me."

Yet sighed the princess: " Nay, then, what means
    Death ?
Some roses fall, clipped by his sharp-ground shears,
Withered and shrinking from his spectral touch,
In earliest bloom. Say, what is Death, Sabrina ?
There gleams the bridle-path among our rocks,
Still wet and rill-like from a sudden shower,
A-winding headlong to the misty vale.
Men seek the hamlet thus ; at will return,
Retracing every footprint in the sod ;
But Death's a steeper path we tread perforce
To duskier realms, down to the cruel grave.
I've mused on this—a-many, many times,
And my chilled soul recoils ! Might Hubert stand,
As oft when, both, we turn to play, and I
Make feebler feebleness for very joy,
So, gazing up, he'll stretch his arms as props

THE APOSTLE OF THE ARDENNES

Lest I should slip or stumble—well, perchance,
Perchance, I say, my fears might then wax less;
Perchance, perchance. . . . Alas! that here is none
To hold me up and lead my tottering steps,
And brace my heart with words of holy faith.
Our home's well famed for wassail and for mead,
For gallant joust and merry tourney-strife;
We mock at priestly warnings—but, methinks,
Faith is a staff folks scarce may need in health,
Yet they who 're old, or haply sick, or lame,
Grope sore for it."

"Sweet lady, here's a maid,
A Saxon damsel, sailed across the sea
From Anglia's shore—that late has joined your court,
Yet lisps our parlance bravely."

"What would she?"

"Your smile, princess. Blind sit we here, deprived;

THE APOSTLE OF THE ARDENNES

But with it need no sunshine for our warmth.
I pray you, cheer us.   Trust me, durst she sing,
Slow roused, she'd chant some strange and saintly stave
Which haply might bring healing to your pain.
Serious is she of speech—a martyr's soul—
Heedless of worldly joys—for this we chide her.
If she but please you, I no more will chide!"

"Yea, bid her come," quoth Floriban.

                                                             But when
The maid obedient stood, with timid air—
Leaving her fellow girls, as some wild bird
That from the feathered crowd of comrades flies
To carol on a distant bough, alone—
The princess sat, with grave averted face,
And gazed from out her turret casement high,
Across the plain of green and sunlit land,
Toward the sombre forest of Ardennes.

Thus ran the rune.

THE APOSTLE OF THE ARDENNES

"A little pilgrim came across the wold
When ice and snow had faded on our hills;
Her eyes were bright as are the sparkling rills,
Her yellow hair as dandelion gold.
'Hast thou no songs,' we said, 'no songs to-day?'
'Yea, one,' quoth she, 'I learned it on the way.'

'Sing, little pilgrim, sing; the land is fair;
Lay down thy cockle shell, thy cloak and shoon.
This world is sweet, and thou shalt gather soon
The honied joys that wait thy coming there.
Then sing.' 'Yea, hearken,' quoth she: 'here's my
    song:
Who travels heav'nward, finds the journey long.'

'Long, little pilgrim? Long, for such as thou?
While hoary travellers still most patient wend
O'er plain, through thicket, seeking ne'er an end?'
The morning sun was on her lips and brow,
With ringing voice upon her way went she:
'Some deem it brief; the way's o'er-long for me.'

THE APOSTLE OF THE ARDENNES

' Dear little pilgrim, hark! the woods, full-brimmed
With bells of blue, chime to the song of birds.'
' I hear my Lord; He calls my heart, His words
More tender than the nightingale has hymned.
I fain would hasten; yea, I must away;
Night cometh; long and weary is the way.'

' Stay thou the night, if that thy path lie far,
Lest darkness thee encompass and affright.'
' Nay, my Lord waits me. He my steps will light
Through yon black tent; my lamp His evening star;
' Twixt rising mists He'll stretch His hand, and say:
Welcome, poor pilgrim, from thy stony way.'

' Tis true; the pebbles cut thy childish feet.'
' This should I grudge? For us upon the cross
His body hung, our wondrous gain His loss,
His tears our grace, His wounds our promise sweet,
Our life His death Who taught my heart the song:
I travel heav'nward, though the road seem long."

THE APOSTLE OF THE ARDENNES

      And when was done the rune—
The strange and solemn strain to silence dropt—
Still sat the princess, with averted face,
And gazed from out her turret casement high,
Across the plain of green and sunlit land,
Toward the sombre forest of Ardennes.

III

How, in pursuit of a milk-white hart, Prince Hubert found himself alone in the far depths of the forest. How he there beheld a divine vision, and was commanded to renounce his former life, and to seek out the holy Lantbert at Maestricht.

III

A royal hart for royal Hubert's bow!
May luck mark out the track, and speed the hunt!
Jocund, the prince fares forth this merry morn,
And pricks his steed, and calls the huntsmen on,
For very cheer and allegresse of sport.

"Good Friday shall it be! ay, in good sooth,
A venturesome gay Friday—such, pardie,
As bids hot summer shrink to nothingness
Her parching roll of close and idle months,
For memory of some perfect hours. Fair Dian!
Chief guardian goddess of these Ardennes woods,
In grace of thee, if thou but grant success,
To-night be our bold deer-hounds garlanded!
And ye, forgotten votaries of the chase,

THE APOSTLE OF THE ARDENNES

Fauns, demigods, whose brawny sun-kiss'd limbs
Crept 'mid green ilex on the Grecian hills
For slaying of the leopard or the wolf—
Ride with us, prosper us! Why, where's the better
In earth or heaven than, borne by breath of Spring,
Skimming the short turf, breezy skies o'erhead—
With steady seat, sure eye, and lusty mind,
And voice that thrills at eager bay or cry—
To hunt the deer, the fleet-foot kingly deer,
Whom none may target save a kingly hand,
Whose skin is regal shroud—a gallant quarry!"
So, with a shout, he waved his hunting cap,
And rode a-gallop o'er the castle bridge,
And down the slope, out to the open plain,
Wending betwixt the copse's greenery,
First of the hunt, as well befitted one
Who must in all things lead; while blast of horns,
And thud of hoofs, quick, multitudinous,
And laughing voices, followed him apace,
With many a joyous song of venerie.

THE APOSTLE OF THE ARDENNES

(Perchance 'twas echo of those stirring songs,
That bade Sabrina tune her kindred call.)

      "Away to the forest!
        Blow, hunter, thy horn!
      Away to the forest
        In the glow of the morn—
Then 'ware, 'ware, 'ware, look ye there, look ye there!
For the king of the forest shall fall to our snare.

      Away through the forest,
        To follow the chace;
      Adown the green forest
        Come gallop apace!
Then 'ware, 'ware, 'ware, look ye there, look ye there!
For the king of the forest's a prize that is rare."

Yet presently the clamorous voices dropt
To earnest silence where the greenwood thickened,
And narrow grew the way—while he, the leader,

THE APOSTLE OF THE ARDENNES

Ever impetuous, spurring fiercely on,
Breasted the forest fringe as one that loves
Its chill familiar dusk of boundlessness.
Yea, so a gallant swimmer takes the sea,
And thus an eagle strikes the loftier air.

Sudden he drew a breath for frantic joy,
But made no sign. Yonder, where arching boughs
Roofed in the verdant floor that seemed an aisle
'Neath some cathedral's vaulted canopy—
There, where smooth grass was laid in tempting path,
With stunted thicket and sparse undergrowth
Frayed to a meagre fringe on either side,
Paled to grey distance far as eye could peer—
Behold a snow-white form ! Softly it trod,
Most leisurely, in dainty ease secure—
A deer of points, a hart of fullest years,
With antlered head but now dipt low to browse,
Now raised to sun-speck'd leafage ; pulling down
And nibbling buds at will—a fearless beast,

THE APOSTLE OF THE ARDENNES

In conscious innocence and perfect rule,
With space untrammelled of a fertile realm,
Ignoring any traitorous near approach
Of man, the world's worst foe to gentle things.

But, as the prince drew nigh yon grassy line,
The hart, with swiftness born of liberty,
(Though seemingly in mild and ambling pace,)
Moved lightly on awhile, then turned and gazed
With melting look toward its rash pursuer;
Next, leaped in bounds upon the forward path
That, winding, sought the bracken, hidden there
To peep again, meandering in and out
As might some clear and slender water-course
Made green by thick-leaved cresses from beneath.
And Hubert followed, urging on his steed.
But, presently, among the beeches' stems,
(For this was sylvan depth,) the track died out,
Broke off, forgot by Nature's restless touch
When for some 'broidery bright she grew more keen—

THE APOSTLE OF THE ARDENNES

A green thread lost in meres of hyacinth
Close rippling at the foot of giant trees,
Where blue-bells went a-nodding up the bank,
To waste themselves in further seas of blue
Wide ranged o'er winter store of dry dead leaves.
There, in flower midst, again the creature stayed,
With turning backward glance of tender eyes.

Yet dares he on—the hunter—yea, alone,
Out-distancing his knightly company,
And steeds, and hounds, and varlets of the chase.
Naught recks Prince Hubert of these wilds untrod,
Of comrades dropt from hearing and from sight,
Of danger nigh; stubborn his rage of sport
That soon must leave him, beggared of all help,
Lost in the thickness of the weird Ardennes.

On, on, and ever on, they race. They fly.
Foremost the hart; the horse, less sure of step,
More ponderous, crashing through the mazy woods,

THE APOSTLE OF THE ARDENNES

Foaming at mouth, with trappings torn of thorns,
And flanks blood-streaked to red; while he, the
    rider,
Half blind by many a spike or bramble wound,
Reels, bruised of cumbrous boughs on every side.
On, swiftly on; with gliding easy grace
The hart speeds in and out among the stems,
Threading dim galleries and tortuous ways,
O'er far for spear, too nigh to count as lost,
And still defying that persistent pride,
Which ne'er a foe had quelled or conquered yet,
Nor yet was yielding.

                      All at once, the screen
Of firs and yews fast-linked in wilderness—
Where scarce a mid-day sun might delve to cleave
The swarthy boughs with misty warming rays—
Oped of itself and parted, to show clear
A broad free space. There Earth of old upheaved,
Hurling grey rocks and boulders as in sport,

THE APOSTLE OF THE ARDENNES

Which Time since decked with patches of soft moss.
There birchen saplings tapered slim, and shook
Their head-dress silvered as are moonlit clouds;
And, in the midst of all—yea, in one place—
The great stones gathered to an eminence,
Piled on each other in fantastic guise;
While, to the base of this most natural altar,
April brought homage of white violets,
Pale primaveres in dimpled yellow cloak,
Enpurpled pansies, wind-flowers snow-betipt,
Gold celandine, and daisies painted red,
With tender grasses and broad festive leaves.

Swift on yon stony stair-way leaped the hart,
And forthwith clomb unto the highest place,
Firm-footed and unslackening in its course.
Then for the third time turned, and stood and
    gazed
Upon that vengeful foe, who yet pursued,
Who fain had dealt out instant cruel death.

THE APOSTLE OF THE ARDENNES

Yea, as the deer so turned, behold a light,
A mighty light about its antlered head!
Lo! 'twixt the velvet of the branching points,
A gleaming Cross that blazed with lambent rays,
Dulling the sky's midday, and, on the Rood,
A figure crowned with thorn and crucified—
Our Lord the Christ.

                     At this most wondrous sight,
The rider—checked in headlong quest, as struck
By some quick lightning shaft sped straight from
    heaven—
Drew hasty rein; his 'frighted beast reared high,
And, sentient as himself, for terror quaked,
While he, the prince, did fling himself to earth.
There sought he now to kneel, in frenzied stound,
Nor could find accent for his palsied tongue,
But silent bent, in lone and lowly state,
And clasped his hands in prayerful attitude,
And sank his shamèd head upon his breast,

THE APOSTLE OF THE ARDENNES

His mind o'erwhelmed.   While Time itself stood still,
Silencing space.

                      For down the awestruck glade
A warm wind passed but sighed not, and no bird
Durst sing, and ne'er a woodland creature moved
Nor stirred, but in their nests the pigeons stayed,
Uncooing, and the swallow paused in flight,
Seeking no midge, and, 'mong the verdant banks,
Conies, field-mice, and wild brown partridges,
Stopt in their gambols; and no cricket chirped.

Till burst a voice upon the listening realm,
In beauty most majestic, far beyond
All richest sound of earth, so the bright air
Seemed shook with glory, as when sudden pours
A mighty crimson flood on chill grey dawn.
It pealed as thunder that o'er quiet lakes
Rolls unexpected, caught by rocky haven
And carried on from mountain peak to peak,

THE APOSTLE OF THE ARDENNES

More clear for hush of storm.   Such tone sublime,
We deem, is by the enchoired seraphim
From holiest holy echoed through the spheres.

And this the message, these the warning words :

" How long, O Hubert, shall thy course endure,
Slaying for pastime hurtless woodland beasts,
All else of life forgetting in thy lust?
Turn to thy God ere that it be too late,
Or Hell's abyss shall gape, and thou fall in ! "

Then spake the hunter, bowed to earth :

         " Dread Vision
Vouchsafed to me, of holy mystery ;
A sinner deep repenting, thy behest
I meekly wait.   Speak, Lord, and I obey."

So pealed God's thunder on his ear once more :

THE APOSTLE OF THE ARDENNES

"Unto my servant Lantbert shalt thou go;
Haste thee to Maestricht—ask and do his bidding."

The mystic voice dropt on the limpid air.
The glory faded into empty day.
A light breath, lifted from the whispering trees,
As though some doves' wings fluttered and outspread,
Crept softly round the hoary moss-grown rock
Where late the hart had stood.

                        Yet Hubert knelt,
And clasped his hands in prayerful attitude—
His shamèd head sunk low upon his breast—
Unmindful that the sun, whose golden keel
Ploughed the blue main of heaven, had drifted low
Westward, more ruddy-disked, athwart the boughs
That yonder made a tracery delicate,
Because the great oaks were but scarce in leaf.
And when at last he rose, of former strength
Seemed he bereft, his body strangely fagged

THE APOSTLE OF THE ARDENNES

By lassitude, though urged by power divine
That armed him cap-à-pie with steeled resolve,
As though new knightliness were granted him.
Then, at his step, that crushed the last-year leaves,
His faithful steed came whinnying to his hand,
While out the thicket leaped his dog, brave hound
And rare, most priceless for the chase, and known
To fame and history's page—Souyllard by name—
Yet haply best of worth for love he bore
Unto his master, to whose breast he sprang,
O'erwhelmed by joy, with eager uncouth paws
Upraised, and ardent tongue, and barks and yelps,
More daring that the prince, who oft had spurned
Or chid him for such venturesome delight,
Spake nothing, gazing out from shining eyes
Fraught with strange comprehension newly learned.

At last—the bridle rein slung on his arm—
Went Hubert, slowly and afoot, to trace
Some homeward path across the verdant wilds

THE APOSTLE OF THE ARDENNES

More thickly wove at every forward step.
Ne'er could he guess how he had entered in,
Or reached that open space now sudden missed.
In vain his hunting horn he blew—again—
And yet again with deep stentorian breath.
A ghostly silence mocked him—yet a blast—
Not even an echo answered desolate.
Dead bracken tangled at his horse's feet,
Long-fronded, russet brown, while, from far shades,
Perplexing alleys oft enticed him, though
Their boskage closed, repellent as a shield.
And many burrows in the hillocked grass
Scarce showed their snares and pitfalls through the
    dusk—
(Declining day, resembling age, ignores
The deepest shadows and the keenest lights,
Cloaking all landmarks in its crepuscule.)

Wearied, he mounted, slowly rode a while,
Pricking with spur the good steed's bleeding flanks,

THE APOSTLE OF THE ARDENNES

For hope to prove the beast more wise than man;
Till stubborn stood the creature, as to ask:
Nay, whither urgest me, and who shall know
The mind of him that wots it not himself?

Then presently did Hubert cease to strive,
And sank, dejected, on the mossy sward,
Beside a trickling water thread, so thin
It scarce might earn the name of brook or stream;
There gave his horse loose rein to pace and graze
In semi-liberty. But Souyllard dragged
His suffering body nigh unto his lord,
With downcast air, and tail that sought the ground,
And speaking eyes of human pathos quite—
A comrade dumb, yet granting sympathy—
So laid a huge paw on his master's knee.
Thus, the brave partner of that sombre hour
The prince bade share such meagre food as lay
To hand within his 'broidered saddle-bag,
Trusting the morrow's need might bring its meed.

THE APOSTLE OF THE ARDENNES

And presently—as darkness curtained them
On broad and grassy bed with ferny pillow—
He threw one arm around the smooth white head
So near his own, and, by this faithful squire,
Slept peacefully until the dawn of day.

He woke. His errant mind, in sleep's domain,
Had rambled through a forest spirit-planted,
Thick-leaved with memories sweet. His half-closed eyes,
Still dreamful, might not quickly burst the thrall
Of yon warm South by vagrant thought evoked—
Cradle and garden of the tenderest years—
Fair Aquitaine! There, in his father's realm,
Stretched fertile valleys, furrowed green with vines,
Specked radiantly by rosy almond boughs,
Nigh the blue ocean line that lapped the shore;
While, 'twixt the blossomed fields and sapphire skies,
Another sea ran broadly—ridge on ridge
Of billows crested white, from east to west—
The mighty mountain line of Pyrenees.

THE APOSTLE OF THE ARDENNES

        Ay, now the sea-sound lingered in his ears
As in the treasured shells that children hold,
And throbbed and sang through dreams, and caught
    the trick
Of his dear father's voice—his father, who
Beset by wars and murmuring of wars
Had sent him—Hubert—as a little child
Forth to a northern court for safety sake,
But was his father still, with loving heart,
Nor chilled by distance, nor by courtly laws,
Toward heir of throne and race. . . .

                       Alas! he woke,
And once again his wide eyes saw dismayed
Around him grouped the wizard forms of trees,
In serried ranks and close battalions drawn,
Wearing the grey coat of the morning mist,
As though some forest king had marshalled them
For first saluting of the rising sun.
And, one by one, the great boughs loomed more clear,

THE APOSTLE OF THE ARDENNES

With cobwebs silver-touched, in dancing light,
And sweet-voiced birds sang matins from high towers,
And squirrels chased each other up and down
The huge gnarled trunks, or leaped from branch to
    branch
For buoyancy of life—and, on the ground,
Busy of errand, tiny beetles crept.

Then all that day, the prince, vain-wandering, went,
Seeking an outlet from his leafy prison,
Most heavy-hearted, knowing not if east,
Or west, or north, or south, his rightful way,
An hungred in that fearsome loneliness,
Where natural beauty made the dungeon walls
But more perverse.
                      Only at eventide
His weary steps drew to a lowly hut
That was a charcoal burner's.   From red logs,
Pale clouding smoke upcurled as might a prayer,
Or hymn of praise, that seeks God's quiet sky

THE APOSTLE OF THE ARDENNES

Beyond our thorn-grown world. And, at the threshold,
Upon a rude bench sat a grandam sere,
Who from her distaff drew the rugged thread
Betwixt brown knotted fingers. Thus she crooned—
It was a song that had nor first nor last—

> " Year in and year out,
> Here I sit and mind my wheel.
> Life is but a turning reel,
> Life is but an earthen clout,
> Life is but a flaxen thread
> Woven for the funeral bed—
> Year out and year in,
> Sit I at my wheel and spin."

Then craved the wanderer lodging and a meal,
And those poor folk, who owned no best to give,
Proffered with homage meek such slender all
As serfdom might dispose. So twilight fell.
And he, the prince, who, with a great content
Received some frugal food, now stood alone,

THE APOSTLE OF THE ARDENNES

Outside the hut, where but a sparse weird fringe
Of fir-trees decked the hill, and thence gazed far,
In silent company of teeming thoughts,
Across the dip of the grey naked heath,
Toward the wide space of an unknown land.

Behold! a broad plain which the frolic wind
Would fain keep outlined—though Night's jealous shade
Crept o'er it with a veil of blinding crape
In her spread arms—a broad and slumberous plain
Where hamlets lay in hollows, inky blots
Lit by no spark, though here and there a crag,
Crowned castle-wise, put forth its flaring beacon,
Vaunting such hospitality as knights bestow
One to another. All o'erhead, God's dome
Shone star-besprinkled, as a good man's soul
Wears deeds of mercy. Yea, and, while he looked,
In Hubert's breast the budding new resolve
Sprang to great height, a Jacob's ladder, aimed
From earth's low palisade to heaven's high wall.

THE APOSTLE OF THE ARDENNES

"Myself," quoth he, "myself will make the depth
Of this black sodden world a star-lit realm.
Swarth is life, formless; here and there, perchance,
The glow-worm flame of us who are the great,
While these, the poor, choke, drowned in night—who knows
But they too should wear heaven's bright livery,
As do the rainpools? See! my life begins.
My will shall be to drag men from the mire—
Mine own good deeds the magnet—so all tongues
Shall cry: what giant strength is this that bears,
Like to a torch, the name of God, through clouds
And storms and darknesses of time, until
He hold it safe on high? Thus, men that would
Enkindle some great war, and set alight
A province, take the burning blazing wood
From league to league across the murky ways
Unto the highest peak. And Floriban,
My Floriban, shall, from her sheltered nook,

THE APOSTLE OF THE ARDENNES

Dawn likewise forth, in modest gleam to shine.
True women—this is said—reach angel-ward
One slender hand; the other lifts the poor.
Yet, as she moves, her eyes shall watch my course."

So spake he who had never learned to pray:
"Thy will, O Lord, Thy will, not mine be done,"
While through the pauses of his speech there strayed
A murmuring cadence from the smoke-bound hut,
Where moved the crone—and oft the mocking wind
Upon the hillside caught the sombre lilt,
And flung it to the pines.

                         "Year in, year out,
I sit and mind my wheel—year out—year in—
Life's but a flaxen thread—a thread—I spin—"

So fitful moaned the crone, so moaned the wind.
And he, the prince, turned back and bowed his head
To the low lintel of the log-made hut,

THE APOSTLE OF THE ARDENNES

And lay, impatient, chafing at slow hours,
Until the dawn with saffron streaked the east.
Then mounted steed and rode to Maestricht town.

While, as he rode, across the windy heath
Were borne to him glad chimes of Easter morn,
Rising from some poor chapel of the plain,
Most scant of voice yet earnest in appeal.
Perchance white angels, having rolled away
The stone that lay against his heart's shut door,
For sake of their dear Lord let daylight in.

"Christ, Christ is risen," clanged the little bells:
"Risen the Christ upon this Easter morn;
Risen is He that died upon the rood—"

Thus sang the little bells in unison,
As rode Prince Hubert straight to Maestricht town.

IV

How Prince Hubert returned from Maestricht, and mourned for Floriban.

IV

"The next thing do."

     Such rede the prelate gave,
In his broad oaken hall at Maestricht town—
Green-meadowed Maestricht on the silver Maas—
High-crenelled Maestricht on the winding Maas.

"The next, the nearest thing—a valiant saying;
The meanest of thy duties veers to noblest
If God shall for thy hand's reach rule it. Go!
Pluck from the dust some common daily charge
As 'twere a diamond—princes ply a task
More toilsome than their fellows'—set it high
Among the jewels of thy royal crown,
Or in the plumage of thine iron helm.

THE APOSTLE OF THE ARDENNES

Too oft we'd choose God's bidding if but He
From His high heaven would bend a willing ear
To learn where our good pleasure lies to-day.
Start not, O gracious Hubert! Have I spelt
Thy hidden thought in o'er-rough manuscript?
Thou wouldst, methinks—a second king of day—
Beam on our unlit world, beneficent
Yet tyrannous, and scorching hot to boot,
Granting thy sovereign wealth to helpless hinds
As to their betters—so the brave sun glows
Impartial on all just and unjust folk,
Placed by our Lord in haughty realms which it
In turn controls. Proud orb! that may not shine,
Nor speed one shaft of gold, beyond His will,
Nor but for His wise permit warm our earth,
While, day by day, it wakes the ruddy east,
And westward dies. Likewise, the queenly moon,
The quivering stars, the deep tumultuous sea,
Smooth flowing rivers, and broad clouds above,
The rushing unseen wind, the lightning's flare—

THE APOSTLE OF THE ARDENNES

All mightier motive powers than man—obey,
Unquestioning of His (their Maker's) aim,
Content by mere docility to prove
His glorious gamut of omnipotence."

Thus, in the great oak hall at Maestricht town,
Had Lantbert said.

                      To him the prince replied:
"So henceforth will I, good my father, seek
Through plain quotidian cares to work the will
Of Him that rules the stars and insects both.
Yet thou, when—like to Christ, who overthrew
The money-changers' tables in the Temple—
Thou in the Campine marshland, far away,
Didst teach the willow-workers Christian truth,
Dragging to earth their heathen altar-slabs,
Maiming their senseless images—how then?
Thine was a splendid quest. New enterprise,
Combat perchance, and dangerous journeying,

THE APOSTLE OF THE ARDENNES

Enriched thy mission with a thousand joys—
Would I were thou!"

                      "God gave the task, my son.
The wild sheep of my fold claimed shepherd's care.
Unlike to thee, I own no earth-spun ties;
So, haply, through the desert wastes He trod,
I yet may track the footsteps of our Lord,
Following such arid path, till time shall come
When holy martyrdom for 'nearest' thing
Lie close to hand and heart, a welcome crown—
Sprung from the very slimmest of those thorns
Which pierced my Master's brow, to blossom out
Snow-white and pure round this unworthy head.

"Yet, can we know? See yonder light-made raft,
Fraught with huge pine-logs from the swarthy woods,
Manned by two striplings—how it swirls 'mid stream,
Caught by the quick-curved eddies treacherous!
Say, shall it sink or swim? Shall one lad die?

THE APOSTLE OF THE ARDENNES

One live? or neither? Haply both! God rules;
We guess not what a moment may bring forth.
Let all work on as men, with manly heart,
And seek not overmuch to carve or mould
Dreams of the future borne on thistledown."

Thereafter Hubert rode back to his own,
Well armed by Lantbert's care 'gainst thief or wolf,
His guide the river for awhile, that lay
Low as a wounded dragon, 'mong the reeds
And osier beds, with glinting shimmering scales—
A type of pagan glory, fettered, prone—
While high against the mid-day skies of blue,
A cross of stone uprose, white, sinless, strong,
Marking the tower of that palatial hall
Where sat good Bishop Lantbert, fain to grant
Counsel and dole to every soul in need.

Now, as he rode, his face set resolute
Toward Ardennes, looming darkly in the west,

THE APOSTLE OF THE ARDENNES

With joyful beat the rider's heart was lift,
Glad as the steed which neighed to find itself
On homeward track.   Content's an hour-glass
Where run the sands of Time o'erfast and free,
And Hubert mused: "Well spake the saintly man
Who urged me back to Louvain's court, to her,
Louvain's sweet daughter—gentle Floriban!"
And oft he smiled unto himself—a smile
Brave as some clambering plant bred by the fire
Of ingle-nook that warms an outer wall,
So burst to leafage far beyond all peers—
The while his mind prophetic pictures raised,
That bade the moments flit on painted wings.
Soon, soon, the greeting; soon, sweet eyes and lips,
Entreating, love-lorn, should be raised to his;
Soon white arms twain wreathe tight about his neck;
Her voice—fit perfume of such fragrant flower—
Gladden his weary heart.   To her he'd tell—
To her alone—the message Maestricht gave.
Had he not e'er by her been understood

THE APOSTLE OF THE ARDENNES

That was a limpid stream of truth and love,
Where, if he gazed, himself he'd find reflected,
With, sometimes, just a dancing circling gleam,
Keen silvered shaft sprung from her soul's deep well,
To shrine his image without blurring it?

The journey done, he reached the castle gate.
Thick vaporous shades of evening clothed the land,
And hid familiar paths with dusky dews.
Perchance because he called in angry haste,
Doubling th' impatience of his hunting horn,
To bid the drawbridge lower, or that he rode
Swift past the warders—idle frightened loons
Who staggered forth, half sleeping and half dazed,
Barren of words of question or of joy—
Yea, haply, while he clattered, careless, swift,
Across the silent courtyard, which, for sure,
Had lacked the master's eye too long already,
He marked no change, nor noted aught as wrong.
The pallid faces of his serving-men

THE APOSTLE OF THE ARDENNES

He waved aside, as they were phantom wisps.
Then laughed aloud. What! had they deemed him
    dead,
Pillowed a-many nights on ferny couch
Of innermost Ardennes? So flung the reins
To one, he cared not which, and sprang to ground,
Bidding another look to Souyllard's needs,
And stable the good horse. Then elbowed past,
Rough as of wont, and sought the inner court:
Floriban's garden.

        As he went, he saw,
By fret of wind laid low, on flagstones stretched,
A pale Lent lily, and he bent him down,
Fearing to bruise the flower with careless foot,
And, seeing how that it lay broke off at stem,
He raised it tenderly, so carried it.
Why stood she not there at her casement high,
His lily wife? Upon the stone-built stair
His step rang loud; yet from yon bower came

THE APOSTLE OF THE ARDENNES

No customary welcome answering word,
Or patter of quick feet. Gloomy the dusk;
A strange o'erwhelming pall. Was Floriban
By spell of slumber bound, as seemed the rest?
The very peacocks roosted in the yews;
Silent the thrush 'mid wattled osier prison;
From all grey towers no girlish laugh or song—
But only bats flew out, black arrows sped
Into the twilight, aimed to right or left.

Nay, here's a light within; high tapers burning,
Whose lifting draught has made the arras thrill
And shiver outward to the dark stair gap.
Be this her bower? This awesome crape-hung cell?
There, in the midst, a bed—a bier—stands lone,
Spread for a slender form draped round with white
Of shroud and winding-cloth sepulchral drawn,
Herself more white than is the fairest hedgerow

THE APOSTLE OF THE ARDENNES

When captious Spring mocks her own impulses,
So flings chill snowdrift on all sun-kiss'd buds—
Apple and hawthorn—closing up the eyes
Of heartsease blue and tearful violet.

Yea, from an inner chamber, as the sigh
Of languid rising waves on southern sand,
Hark! the low murmur of the damsels' plaint:

"Wail, wail for her whom Death and Sleep
Have ta'en by either hand, to keep
Henceforth in caverns dark and deep!

To her no red rose-wreaths ye bear;
Her captive shade must ever wear
Death's poppies grey on breast and hair.

Her life three golden threads had spun—
Youth, Love, and Hope—three threads in one;
Now Atropos hath all undone.

THE APOSTLE OF THE ARDENNES

Wail, sisters! where she wanders pale
Our longing arms and voices fail.
Weep, maidens, weep! Wail, sisters, wail!"

Then lapsed the grief to silence for a breath;
But next, from further distance—like the sob
Of storm through moonlit oleander groves,
When every bush or tree in turn gives voice,
Till soon the forest rocks itself and moans—
Gathered the murmur of unquiet pain:

> "Night hath fallen on my heart
> Since I saw my queen depart—
>   (*Vale, vale,* Floriban!)
>
> Kindle dawn and sunset burn!
> She shall never more return—
>   (*Vale, vale,* Floriban!)
>
> Nevermore, O nevermore!
> She hath oped Death's iron door—
>   (*Vale, vale,* Floriban!)

THE APOSTLE OF THE ARDENNES

Went she singing through the way,
As a bride on marriage day?
  (*Vale, vale,* Floriban!)

Could ye not have held her close?
So the thorn-boughs shrine a rose—
  (*Vale, vale,* Floriban!)

Ivy, yew, and cypress tree,
Weep for her and weep for me!
  (*Vale, vale,* Floriban!)

Night hath fallen on my heart
Since I saw my queen depart—
  (*Vale, vale,* Floriban!)"

Then closer drew the prince's footfall, close,
And closer yet, till, nigh the snowy bed,
The broken lily dropt from out his hand,
And fell across the cerements, touching her

THE APOSTLE OF THE ARDENNES

That might not stir nor move her slender hand,
Whose shut lids never throbbed, though he, her knight,
Stood by and gazed on her, with grief as great
As when a stricken king views from some cliff
His kingdom sacked and all his warriors slain.
Mute stood he — wounded to the strong heart's core.
Pain, as it welled, gave forth nor moan nor cry,
But hot tears rolled from out his anguished eyes,
And hard he wrung his hands in bitterest woe.

Last, bent he down and kneeled, and pressed his face—
His wet wan face—against the silken couch,
And kiss'd with hungered lips the strands of hair
That held his aching heart in fief as when
His wrists were bound thereby for mirthful play;
While, through the twilight, winging upward flight
From life's great ruin, sprang the litany

THE APOSTLE OF THE ARDENNES

Of one who ne'er to Heaven had raised a hand,
Nor sped a shaft of prayer.

      "Thy will, O Lord,
Thy will, Thy will—not mine—be done, dear Lord—
Not mine, not mine."

      The pleading words came fast,
As founts of blood drawn from that bursting heart.
He prayed. And she, whose lips were locked in death,
Lay still—a sweet saint wrought in marble form—
Nor answered; nay, nor could have heard the prayer,
Or from far shades her wraith had surely come,
Breaking such bonds as bind beyond our ken,
Because of that great love which motioned her.
So prayed he till e'en prayer waned on his lips,
And he grew faint for weariness of grief;
Then raised a hand and crossed her where she lay,
Where prone she lay in stainless silent sleep,
Wife of his youth, wife of his home and love,
Lover and queen and slave, ay, all in one.

THE APOSTLE OF THE ARDENNES

Thus, with his tears for baptism on her face,
His warm tears dropping on her frozen face,
God's own cross signed he o'er her brow and breast,
God's holy sign for all eternity.

Then, sudden, saw Sabrina with the babe.

For she, Sabrina, on whose lips had failed
Intended speech, held in her sheltering arms
A bud of life, whose blue eyes flickered pale,
While one small hand strained out, as though to
    plead
Itself not fully guilty of disaster.

But quickly rose the prince, perturbed, in wrath;
Drew back a step; he, likewise, lacked for words,
And, as in trance, with cold stare fixed his son.
Yet presently, deep sighing, thus spake he:

"Haste, seek some wandering friar, or any such
Ordained to holy Christian rites, that this

THE APOSTLE OF THE ARDENNES

Be numbered lamb of Christ ere one more hour
Loom heavy o'er a life so frail. God's fold
Shall stand to Floribert—who is all beggared
Of mother-love—for mother's arms and knees,
Those natural bastions 'gainst the bitter world ;
The Church shall be to him sole nursery-ground,
With praying monks for playmates, and their chaunt—
Harmonious plain-song—make his lullaby.
God's blessing falls perchance most tender-wise,
'Stead mother's kiss, upon the motherless."

V

How Prince Hubert dwelt for ten years in lowliness and solitude.

V

Deep in green-leaved retreat the hermit sat;
A vellum scroll loose-laid across his knee.
Here was quaint lore, set rich with scarlet ink,
Enflowered of that mellifluous tongue as seemed
Warm-steeped in sunshine of the rhythmic South—
Ne'er wearied of, because a mother tongue.
Yet sometimes would his calm eyes truant turn,
For seeking knowledge from great Nature's self,
So gazing upward to the umbrageous woods
Of this familiar spot in fair Ardennes,
Whose verdure made palatial canopy,
Roof beyond roof, raised high o'er yon poor hut
That craved the solace of their suzerain strength,
As when a field-mouse creeps beneath the hedge.

Ten years—slow-meted years—ten golden coins

THE APOSTLE OF THE ARDENNES

Given by God's mercy for the ransoming
Of one brave soul. Ten quick receding years—
Short span wherein to lift a mind from earth!
Had Time indeed struck on this world's clock-face
A decade's knell? or, with his lightning touch,
Flashed forth ten moments? Lo! our years are
    like
To ripe red fruit which, as a youth in sport,
He of the sickle shakes from trees of Life
Through mockery of his helpless vassal, man,
In that the balls roll swiftly out of reach.
Next juggles he therewith, till we, poor fools,
We know not if they fly from his deft hands,
Or slacken—for deceiving of our eyes!

"Ten years." Such was the dictate Lantbert gave,
Whom, swayed by grief, again the prince sought out
At Maestricht, and, disciple-like, obeyed:

Ten years to dwell, king of a hermit's cell,

THE APOSTLE OF THE ARDENNES

Hid in the closest core of hunting ground,
Hushed by soft crooning of the rustling oaks,
Quenching thine ill and fever of despair
By prayerful silence, while thy naked feet
Tread sombre paths where, lord of steeds and hounds,
With hue and cry, and clanking retinue,
Thou didst pursue the sylvan innocents.
Bend thy proud spirit where it triumphed most,
Relentless, in its carnal rage of sport!
Pluck slender grasses with unweaponed hands
For rest of royal limbs; thy spear, thy knife,
Thine axe, thine arrows—yea, thy conquering lust—
Laid by for aye, Content thine only spoil,
And, as thy rightful chace, that patient trust
Which men win, by much seeking, on their knees!"

Thus the harsh rede. But, when the words were said,
With austere voice, and looks severely ruled
For guardianship, behold! the prelate leaned
Quick to his penitent, and, misty-eyed,

THE APOSTLE OF THE ARDENNES

With sudden outstretch of paternal arms,
And faltering speech: "My son! my son!"—as he
That saw his child, the prodigal, return,
And ran, and fell upon his neck for joy,
Weeping, because joy's cords root deep in grief,
And grief is subtly twist with joy—"My son,"
The good man sobbed, and clasped the other's hands,
And kissed him for farewell and blessing both;
And he—prince Hubert—bowed his head and wept.

Thereafter soon—that consecrate embrace
Yet warm upon his brow—departed Hubert,
Travelling to Aquitaine without delay,
And of his father, the old lion Duke,
Seeking strange grace: that Eudes, the junior born,
Henceforth be heir, and Hubert held as dead,
Disherited, not Esau-like through greed,
Nor forced by fear or grim necessity,
But, like to Christ, forswearing royalty,
And, with such king-ship, purple robes and gold

THE APOSTLE OF THE ARDENNES

And cushioned down for body and for mind.
Yea, e'en as Christ, Who meek bestrode an ass
To enter into proud Jerusalem,
(So gathered scorn from men of might and mark,)
Decried was he, to whom an escort sent
Of noble knights, in gorgeous panoply,
A gilded cavalcade—rich velvet flung
About each starry lance and saddle-bow—
Brought gifts of jewelled coats and scarves and gloves,
And cunning chains strung thick with orient pearl,
Likewise set round with fond parental greeting.
The courtly messengers wagged sapient heads,
Muttering rank treason under breath, to see
The heir of such a broad and leal domain,
His sad wan face by monk-like sable hood
Close-shrouded—ay, a blot on that bright land,
A note of grief amid the jocund music—
Pass on, unheeding all fair gifts and words,
Dust-stained, nor sword nor axe hung at his side,

THE APOSTLE OF THE ARDENNES

Urging his weary palfrey to the palace,
A-stumbling at each pebble on the road.

Already, gay princesses and court dames,
Witting of his—the princely heir's—approach,
Had shook out silks and smiles, and curled their locks,
Each whispering: "Surely thee, dear, he must choose;
Scarce could he otherwise.   Alack ! poor soul—
A widower, handsome, with so young a babe !
Yea, *thou* art born true queen of Aquitaine."
While each within her bosom furtive dreamed :
"'Tis I who'll net him ; without doubt, 'tis I."

But, all he willed being vowed without reserve,
(And still the Bishop's saying writ on heart,)
Northward turned Hubert, and so travelled back,
Leaving the laughing seas and vine-crowned lands,
And all sweet lurings of his father's court,
Northward returning to the dark Ardennes.
Therein he built his hut, and raised hard by

THE APOSTLE OF THE ARDENNES

A cross which, with his own so toilful hands,
He carved of aspen, that atoning tree
Bearing, he deemed, some semblance of himself,
Because, upon the dread and darkened hour
Of Crucifixion, when all nature quailed,
'Twould bow no leaf, but ever syne had shuddered,
And must so quiver till the time of Doom.

There sat he down, beneath the greenwood shade,
And dwelt, while passing days heaped high to moons,
And one by one the pale moons waxed and waned
Piled up to years, and each succeeding year
Peeped primrose-like through snow, and, after summer,
Hung with dull lids 'twixt autumn and cold death,
To drop a-swoon into December's maw.
There, with each year, grew Hubert's brow more smooth,
Because God's patience wiped the harsh lines out,
And his grave eyes as stars of mercy shone
From a serene and holy countenance;

THE APOSTLE OF THE ARDENNES

But while, full-toned, the beard flowed down to reach
His belt of cord, upon his sparser locks
Time's envious finger laid, with hasty touch,
Some threads torn from the white and chilly shroud
That Grief, like Age, can weave for mortal men.

And thus to-day, at peace with all the world,
The hermit conned the secrets of his scroll,
Itself resembling life, half hid, half spread,
Close tracked with writing red as blood, but gold
Touched here and there, for marking of rare
    days
Burnished by good deeds or great happiness.
Oft sat he thus, alone, yet not o'er-lonely;
For, as to all that solitary dwell,
There daily stole beside him, strangely near—
Crouching in converse sweet through twilight hour,
At frugal meals, or pacing step by step
Adown the slumbrous pathways of the wood—
A timid sprite, a presence sensitive,

THE APOSTLE OF THE ARDENNES

Issued from out some dim mysterious cave,
(There born of Silence, Meditation nursed,)
A duplex self, a finer grander soul,
That, ere its twin, had cast off all of earth.
So fugitive this friend, if the light foot
Of some young fawn but brushed the tender grass,
Or if the nested fledglings chirped o'erloud,
'Twould flee back 'frighted to the sheltering copse
Reluctant to return, though sought and wooed.
They that dwell ever with their fellow-men,
Know not the sweetness of such weird companion,
Pure reflex of what's noblest in each mind,
That shall, Egeria-like, be only found
Shrined in the shaded groves of peaceful thought,
Where noise and fret of life may never come.
Yea, some there be, in lofty-tempered mood,
Who seek for mirror heaven's blue canopy,
Gazing persistent at a nobler world,
To gain the holiest portraiture—as he,
Whose task is molten silver to refine,

THE APOSTLE OF THE ARDENNES

Completes his work but when his own face shines
Reflected there: God's image.

                                         Well that thus
The lonely soul clasps hands with purer self,
Perfecting life—life that's a cobweb spun
Down to the daisies from the cloudy heights!

And this the ancient lore that Hubert read:

    Our father Adam, nigh to death,
    Bade call his son—his best-lov'd—Seth.

    "Have come and gone nine hundred years
    Since I awaked to earthly spheres.

    Alas! Till now mine arm held strong
    For woodman's toil the daylight long;

    But, yester-morn, the spade I drave
    Dug deep the trenches of my grave.

THE APOSTLE OF THE ARDENNES

Yon mighty bush I fain would bend
Hath done me hurt and brought mine end.

Dear son, most pure of heart and wise,
Seek out our lov'd lost Paradise.

An angel stands, with flaming sword
To guard the gateway of the Lord.

Near by, the Tree of Life, with flowers
From which sweet oil of mercy pours.

Beg thou for me the merest drain—
The smallest drop—to ease my pain."

Thus Adam, moaning as he lay;
And Seth went sorrowing on his way.

But, when he came to Paradise,
The Tree of Knowledge met his eyes—

That tree whose fruit so ripe and sweet
The serpent tempted Eve to eat.

THE APOSTLE OF THE ARDENNES

And lo! upon the crowning height,
A being seated, robed in light;

His face, all fair to look upon,
Than noonday sun more glorious shone.

The Christ was He—Who promise gave
To Seth our world from sin to save,

And on such day bring Mercy's oil
Adam and all men to assoil.

Thereon, th' archangel gathered three
Small seeds from Life's majestic tree:

"When cold and dead thy father lies
Take thou these grains of Paradise,

And place within his mouth, nor fail
Or e'er he sleep in Hebron's vale."

Thus Michael spake, and Seth obeyed—
For Adam soon to rest was laid.

THE APOSTLE OF THE ARDENNES

Then from the tomb three rods were seen,
Swift saplings, girt about with green.

Untouched they grew till Moses, brought
By angel hand, the green rods sought,

Ordained to pluck, at God's command,
Those boughs that breathed of Promised Land,

To heal the sick, the blind, the lame,
Obedient to His holy name,

To draw pure water from a rock,
And earth's strange knowledge to unlock.

Years passed. The rods lay all unknown;
Then David reigned on Israel's throne,

And journeyed forth in search of them,
For blessing of Jerusalem.

Thus once more did they give, to such
As prayed, sweet healing in their touch,

THE APOSTLE OF THE ARDENNES

But soon, within a pure spring placed,
Were by the King found interlaced—

Three-fold in one—a cedar tree—
Type of the blessèd Trinity.

This David to the Temple bare.
Awhile it spread and flourished there;

Yet lastly felled by Solomon—
As 'twere a bough from Lebanon—

And laid with piles of precious wood
Unto the Temple's glory hewed.

Next stole away, profaned to plank
The bridgeway o'er a common tank,

Where all folks' footsteps heedless went
That to the Temple's gates were bent;

Till Sheba's mighty queen drew nigh,
Who held the gift of prophecy.

THE APOSTLE OF THE ARDENNES

Descending from her car of state,
She lowly did herself prostrate,

Nor stept upon the sacred floor,
But kneeled and worshipped, crying sore:

"Behold the glorious Rood whereon
Shall die for us God's only son!"

Then Solomon set up the tree
Within a holy shrine, to be

Girt round by silver clasps—the same,
Their number thirty—which became

In after age th' accursed meed
Of Judas, for his direful deed.

Yet in the water's depth there lay
A splinter dropt upon the way,

Which wrought such miracles that still
Were cured the sick of pain and ill.

THE APOSTLE OF THE ARDENNES

And thus, for healing power proclaimed,
Bethesda's wondrous pool grew famed.

As came the hermit to these words, and stayed—
With pointing finger on the golden rune—
Lifting his quiet eyes, he sudden saw
Two fur-clad herdsmen rollick down the glade,
Who noisy laughed, with cruel knives in hand,
And bore a bleating kid, while, with full voice,
They trolled a snatch of song which, weed-like, clung
Near to their heathen-nurtured lips and minds.
Naught else they knew—and harshly on the ear
Of him that listened fell the pagan words,
Evoking garish pictures of the past,
Which tears and prayers so fain had blotted out.

"Good Father Pan, we shepherds bring
To thee our tribute offering,
And at thine altar dance and sing.

THE APOSTLE OF THE ARDENNES

The greatest of all goat-herds thou—
With verdant wheat we bind thy brow.
Give us of harvest-gold enow.

Sweet blood of firstlings shalt thou have,
And in the crimson glory lave—
Then save our flock, great father, save!"

Adown the wood the echoing voices died—
"Good Father Pan . . ." with ever the refrain:
"Great Father Pan . . . O hearken, Father Pan!"—
Calling the leering satyrs to their aid,
With him, the Prince of satyrs, first and most,
Whose horns and hooves were linked to godliness,
And he the worthier (because half a brute)
To taste the bleeding sacrifice of brutes,
Himself the lowest form, therefore his cult
Lowest and foullest, and his feasts most lewd.

Adown the wood the jarring voices died.
Thus may at length all heathenesse fade out,

THE APOSTLE OF THE ARDENNES

All savage creeds, and soulless rioting,
To leave unto the tranquil peace of God
The one great Truth that like a forest grows
Each day more wide, more high—primeval sown,
Yet freshly green, new-blossomed with each hour!

But, when the hermit—king of solitude—
All things quiescent save re-wakened thought—
Turned to his scroll, no longer might he read.
His ardent spirit, bursting into wrath,
Chafing as though it ne'er had learned content,
Grew turbulent to wrestle with false gods,
And quell the votaries of blind unbelief.
So laid he down the golden lore, and moved
Some slow steps deeper through the forest shade,
And from the pouch that at his girdle hung
He took a slender store of bread, and stood,
With palms held forth, appealing to the spell
Of summer-softened afternoon; then spake
A few swift words of call.

THE APOSTLE OF THE ARDENNES

                        Behold! there came
From out each dim-lit aisle of that great forest,
Along each path, from every bough or burrow,
From every mossy corner and each roost,
Or swinging nest, or leafy hostelry,
Some creature of the woods: brown thrushes, tits,
Linnets and finches trilling rondels sweet,
Robins and wrens—both winsome fire-bringers—
The merle with yellow beak, the halcyon bird
From pools, where sapphire-like he loved to dive,
While all gay butterflies drew back ashamed
Of their down's dulness. Next, the sparrow hopped
Across the velvet sward with agile feet,
As half forgetful of that ancient curse
Which bound his walk, and bade him evermore
Move fettered; and, unawed, where Hubert stood,
About his head the circling swallow veered,
To brush his robe with sleek far-reaching wing
Or sudden red-flamed glow of ambient throat;
While from wide sycamores the rook down dropt,

THE APOSTLE OF THE ARDENNES

Cawing, and starlings, in a sable flock,
Darkened the sky for hasting hungrily.
But white doves 'lighted, cooing, on the shoulder
That bade them welcome, broad and motionless;
And, o'er the outstretched arms, (firm as the rail
Of some staired balcony, approved for play
And gleeful games of merry boys who slide,
Chasing each other up and down in fun,)
The tawny squirrels, swift as lightning flash,
Flared to and fro, now seizing crumbs for sport,
Now hiding them in fold of sleeve or hood,
Or, bright-eyed, peering up to deeper orbs
That loving-wise gazed down. And, unafraid,
The nuthatch, sleek with blue and yellow dress,
Crept to the hermit's mouth for food and kiss,
And the rose-breasted bulfinch puffed and bowed,
Quaint courtier-like, secure upon his wrist.
Then, from far verdant alleys came the thud
Of the wild red-deer's tread, as, ambling on,
Deliberate, and with haughty head raised high,

THE APOSTLE OF THE ARDENNES

They sniffed the perfumed air and so approached;
Stag, hind, and fawn, a-crowded round about.
With them, the graceful fallow deer in troop,
Eager to press soft muzzles to the hands
That were so kind and so familiar grown,
Or pull, for gentle greed, the woollen robe
That clothed the hermit, in sweet ignorance,
Naught witting of that iron coat of mail
Which tore his flesh beneath, but only taught
By tender touch, and seeking such largesse
As daily he had used them to receive.

Last, as the hot sun westward slowly sank,
They wended back—each creature to its lair;
And on his knees prayed Hubert, till, once more,
Victor of self, he laid his docile will
As gift upon the cross of aspen wood.
And yet he prayed, while Night, like Charity,
Her sombre cloak wide-spread, beneficent,

THE APOSTLE OF THE ARDENNES

Clasped him and all the forest denizens
Within the sheltering spell of her embrace.

ST HUBERT'S PRAYER:

TAKE, Lord, in trust my wandering thoughts, so they
Within Thy saintly satchel may be housed,
At rest, secure, and loth to fall or stray,
Nor by the glamour of vain phantoms roused.

Sheave, Lord, my hopes; tie with Faith's golden string,
Safe in Thy mead where dare no thief come nigh;
Yea, bind my soul to Thine own garnering,
In threshing-time still at Thy feet to lie.

VI

How Prince Hubert was elected Bishop in place of the murdered Lantbert, and thereafter attained to great dignity and power, and ruled long and beneficently.

VI

Men tell that erst a palmer came to Rome,
Dust-stained and worn by travel and by toil,
Yet of right noble face and mien, and scarce
Past youth's fair flower of days.   So meekly there
Stood he aside—his bowed head penitent,
Clad in poor dress, with naked bleeding feet,
And wearied eyes most mild and lowly fixed,
Letting the rough folk elbow as they pleased—
They marked him for the humblest peasant born.
Adown he knelt upon yon floor of stone,
Before the giant semblance of St Peter.
He kissed the bronze that was his journey's goal,
Sighing, in part for memory of old wrongs,
And part because now seemed all journeys done,

THE APOSTLE OF THE ARDENNES

All roads at end, life in a casket hid
Of which he'd lost the key, and, like a child
That dreads the dark and has no heart to stir,
He spread forth helpless hands in search of light.

Awhile he lay, with forehead to the ground,
His brow and beard half swathed in palmer's rags,
His shrouded mind half slumbrous in a trance—
Forgetful whether this indeed were Rome,
Or chill Brabant, or sunny Aquitaine—
Unheeding that he had not tasted food,
Nor rested his sick body as it craved,
A-drooping through excess of weariness.
But sudden—rough awakening from his peace—
Behold! a crowd that seemed not nigh before,
Surging about him with triumphant cries—
Environing, though of protective air,
While leaving space that was a pathway made
By such as clear the footsteps of the great.
Then all at once, and much against his will,

THE APOSTLE OF THE ARDENNES

Uplifted was he by the alien folk,
And borne some distance on, he knew not where.

That morn Sergius the Pope had dreamed a dream.
An angel 'lighted close to his bedside,
And touched him on the arm, so that he woke,
Or deemed he woke. There, in the thrill of dawn,
The white-winged radiant creature drew anear,
With quivering feet poised light above the floor,
And hair of cloud, and eyes like burning stars,
And voice that as a silver horn rang pure,
Crying aloud : that Bishop Lantbert lay
Foul-murdered—far away in Belgic Gaul—
Foul-murdered—bathed in warm and holy blood
Shed for the church and God—Lantbert the good—
The newest martyr pagan hate had made.
Yea, with this cry the angel laid a staff
(An ivory wand that had been Lantbert's own)
Within the withered ivory hand of him
Who held the mystic keys of Peter's realm.

THE APOSTLE OF THE ARDENNES

So bade him rise and straightway quick repair
Unto the great basilica, and seek
The last-come pilgrim to the apostle's shrine,
One princely born, of princely height and mien,
Yet of all men best clothed in humbleness,
Who, and none other, might accounted be
Worthy to fill good Bishop Lantbert's seat,
To preach of love, and risk a martyr's death,
(Because love casts out fear,) and without dread
To rule by justice, treading down all weeds,
But tending such fair growth of piety
As Lantbert sowed at Maestricht for the Lord.

Lo, while yet listened Sergius, o'er his eyes
Faded the angel's wings to space of dawn
That shimmered from pure silver into rose,
Next, golden grew, slanting through doors of heaven,
Yet reached no more the brightness that was gone.

Then Sergius called, and swift his retinue
Gathered about him, all in haste, astonied,

THE APOSTLE OF THE ARDENNES

Donning rich robes of state, while heralds cried,
And trumpeters blew loud a stirring theme.
And wide the palace gates rolled back on hinge,
And gorgeous vestments glittered in the sun,
With banners ruby-bordered held aloft.
And scarlet robes, and purple, thronged the road
As sallied forth the Pope's procession proud;
Lastly himself, borne 'neath a canopy,
The richest point of splendour, iris-hued
Beyond all else, and starred with precious stones.
But, when was reached the house of God, alone
The pontiff chose to make his anxious quest,
Bidding his court keep back, and leave him free.
So passed among rude serfs and untaught folk
Who stumbled, dazed and struck with sudden fear,
Brought from their knees and early orisons.
Yet one poor pilgrim, wrapt in woollen rags,
Lay on the stone, or swooned or lost in prayer,
Or haply dead, while, from his dusty robe,
His bare and blood-stained feet showed forth.

THE APOSTLE OF THE ARDENNES

                                      To him
The Pope went straightway, looking on his face
With such kind smile of greeting as is given
To some lost friend but newly found again.
Next bent, and kissed the pilgrim on the brow,
And laid with trembling touch on those twain hands
Now meekly clasped, but outlined broad with strength
Of one that's conquered oft in fight and field,
The ivory staff by angel herald brought.

Thereat, the priestly crowd rushed upon Hubert,
And lifted him, and bore him from his place;
While the basilica, though wide, fast filled
With folk that, following, saw the pageant wind
Through narrow streets to thread the mighty doors,
And lose itself, a-chaunting all the while,
As may a torrent on the grey hillside,
Eclipsed within a chasm. Lifted was he,
On strong triumphant arms that bore him thence,
Unto the palace. There his sores were washed,

THE APOSTLE OF THE ARDENNES

And he was clad in robes of 'broidered silk,
As well beseemed his princely name and grace.
Moreover, soon, a festal day was claimed,
That Hubert should, by Sergius' willing hand,
Be ordained bishop, consecrate in stead
Of saintly Lantbert—he whose eager spirit
Had reaped its wish, and trod so close and deep
Within the footprints of our Lord the Christ,
That, at a thrust from one most heathen spear,
It straightway passed into eternity,
With ne'er a backward look toward human life.
And still the saying's rife how angels brought
Vestments, that had enwrapt the martyr's limbs,
To clothe the Prince, his friend and meek disciple,
Who, an he chose, were Lord of Aquitaine,
Now that the old Duke's years had come to end—
For he was eldest born.

                    Yea, this is sure:
That when he knelt him down—bishop elect—

THE APOSTLE OF THE ARDENNES

Nigh to the fragrant altar dim in cloud
Of incense, princes of the church around,
And noble priests and dignitaries high,
Whose gorgeous retinues, of church or state,
Thronged spacious aisles and misty colonnades,
Clad in such varied splendour of apparel
As made the floor seem some fair garden spread
With blossoms, set 'mong prismic drops of dew,
Fired by the roseate rising of the sun—
While overhead grand choral harmonies
Wrought sweetest incense for the listening ear,
As 'twere the voice of heavenly companies
Allied to earth this one triumphal day—
He, Hubert, saw beyond the Roman walls,
Beyond the wide Campagna with its dunes
Of grassy soil where shepherds lead their flocks,
Beyond great Alps, those white-capt sentinels
That bar the sunny southland from the north,
Nor let soft chestnut woods and olive groves
Join hands with pine and fir of colder growth.

THE APOSTLE OF THE ARDENNES

His mental gaze, travelling in haste and far,
Across the plains of Gaul and Allemayne,
To further realms that lay familiar spread,
Discerned, hard by the silver winding Maas,
A little knoll, green as the scarf of Hope,
Crowned by sparse dusky trees, among whose roots
The starry aconite and celandine
Peep ready at the first gay call of Spring.
There, daily, was good bishop Lantbert wont
To sit, and patient hear the tale of those
That brought their griefs or troubles to his feet,
Laying them down—as peasants at a shrine
Bring gifts of homely produce, then wend back
With lightened sacks or baskets and light hearts;
For he with wise discernment took of pain
As lessened much the load, bestowing joy
Sometimes, and always tender sympathy.

Deep stirred by memories of that holy man,
Prayed Hubert: " Lord Christ, count Thou also me

THE APOSTLE OF THE ARDENNES

As one of Thine apostles—though the least,
Yet one—" and thus prayed o'er and o'er.

                                                  And after,
When from the doors the great procession wound,
Snow fell as though to carpet every road
With blossoms white, and make the pure robes purer
That vested him, the bishop—white o'er white—
White alb and cope, white stole and mitre white—
By heaven more dazzling wrought, beyond earth's
    glory.
And lo! on lintel, step, and roof, and sill,
A feathery cloth was sudden gently laid,
Unfolded wide to join the mantle clean
That draped the towers and archways, circling them,
Or crept round hoary walls.   Fast fell the snow,
Message of peace, and pledge of holiness,
Wiping out mould and stain as silent acts
Of mercy cover up the print of sin,
And blot out what is dark and foul in man.

THE APOSTLE OF THE ARDENNES

Fast fell the snow.
                    Then, from a hidden street,
Or court, or sanctuary withheld from view,
Arose some children's voices, pure as snow,
That carolled forth into the frozen air—
For time had not gone long past Christmas-tide.

And Hubert, riding close at the right hand
Of Sergius, as became his noble state,
Drew rein, and paused, to listen to the song.

    "When Jesu was a little child,
      He sleep'd on Mary's knee and smiled,
          She rocked Him on her knee;

    (*So pray you hearken, gentles all,*
    And give us cheer in house and hall,)
          She rocked Him on her knee.

    'Noel, Noel,' the angels sung,
    The dumb beasts spake in unknown tongue
         For Benedicite;

THE APOSTLE OF THE ARDENNES

(So pray you hearken, gentles all,
And give us cheer in house and hall,)
    For Benedicite.

The shepherds' flute gave merry sound;
With hollies green they strowed the ground,
    For joy the Christ to see;
(So pray you hearken, gentles all,
And give us cheer in house and hall,)
    For joy the Christ to see."

Thereafter, write the faithful chroniclers,
Prince Hubert journeyed back to his own realm,
And unto Liège, where the dead bishop lay,
Because of that pure death of martyrdom
Transferred his dignity of bishopric.
Also to him the king most gladly gave
Power and possessions, so he freely ruled,
Increased the city, girt it round with walls,
To shrine the fair cathedral of St Lantbert.

THE APOSTLE OF THE ARDENNES

Wise laws he made to guide the citizens,
With rightful justice well administered.
Churches and monasteries builded he,
With much of land and rich appurtenance,
Bravely endowed for glory of the Lord.
And in the Campine land he laboured long
Among the willow workers of the marsh,
Whom Lantbert held for wild sheep of his flock;
Nor left the dwellers of the woods untutored,
But loved them best, so haply drew them best
From out their cramping net of pagan use—
For love is of all lures most powerful.

VII

How, after many years, Hubert, justly named The Apostle of the Ardennes, came to his death.

VII

"Nay, Floribert, I may not rest."

                                       So spake
The aged prelate, journeying with his son,
And with them much of princely retinue,
Across the dusky forest of Ardennes,
Once more, once only.

                          "Nay, I may not rest.
Too soon my body, like a tired steed,
Shall stand loose-bridled at Death's hostelry,
Gallop and ambling fret o'er-past for ever.
Already now—as Moses, who at end
Of long and hoary years beheld with yearning,

THE APOSTLE OF THE ARDENNES

From sad restriction of the mountain verge,
Land which his sight, but ne'er his feet, might roam,
Broad promised land that touched the utmost sea,
Valleys to southward, warm in golden light,
The city named of palm-trees, odorous
For sweetness, and for grace beyond compare—
Yea, e'en as he, the heaven-taught patriarch,
I feel mine hour at hand, and do entreat
That thou take patience while I gaze on this,
My Canaan here, a while, a little while.
Knows not each heart some milk and honey realm,
Unreached, ungrasped, dim outlined in the mist?
Thrice blessèd he who, scarce in sight of it,
Yet is content that others, following close,
Outstripping him, shall reap the happy fields
Where he but traced faint visions through the blue.
And I would loose, at bidding of my God,
Whate'er of love of life yet clings to me;
So warriors may unbuckle ere they sleep
Those plates of steel that were their noon-tide glory.

THE APOSTLE OF THE ARDENNES

"'Twas here, in youth's hot prime, I tarried once,
Impatient of past joys, and keen to mould
The future, like to clay, what shape I would.
Ay, then was I so eager! All seemed mine:
This shadowy plain, that distance, clasped within
My fingers' hold; the very stars of heaven,
With lesser gems to boot, carved clear for me!
See, how this noble Rood the wide ledge crowns
Whence silver pines o'ertower the tranquil vale—
But yester-year I bade the woodman hew it,
To be a landmark for the country side.
Here erst, a hut, most rudely built of logs,
Sheltered thy father through the night. Methinks
I hear yon old crone mutter at her wheel!
Yea, when she'd fed me with some savoury mess,
I trod this narrow path, and dreamed, and dreamed,
Of glorious rule—a power unlimited—
All men's obedience to my potent sway—
Triumph at first, and next a conquest new;
With ever by my side my Floriban!

THE APOSTLE OF THE ARDENNES

" My little Floriban ! 'Tis said a wife
Should stand as high as her lord's heart—no more ;
Albeit, methinks, whether tall-grown or short,
She shall besiege and storm that heart so surely,
With cordon of her twain white arms, that it—
The captive castle—swift capitulates !
Thou never knew'st thy mother, Floribert ;
Else had she soothed and dandled on her knee
The helpless babe herself had brought to life,
And crooned to thee soft lullings—whispering close
An hundred pretty mysteries in thine ear,
For amulets, to wear through sullen times
Of childhood, youth, and manhood, talismans
To keep thee safe of danger till old age.

" A dove amid her doves, I saw her first,
At Louvain, in her father's tilting-yard—
For Dagobert was fain to have her near—
A white bird on her shoulder, one on wrist,
While one sought honey from her laughing lips.

THE APOSTLE OF THE ARDENNES

(I vowed I'd rival him!)   And, presently,
She laid her slender hand within mine own,
That thrilled and quivered quick at touch of it—
A roseleaf in the rough and sinewy palm
Of him, Hubert the Hunter, who, men said,
Drew daily breath but to slay gentle things.
She loved me, Floribert—she loved me well."

Thereat he turned him from his folk, and moved
With slow and painful step unto the cross,
And kneeled upon the turf, and spread his arms,
And, tender-eyed, gazed o'er the broad domain;
Till they that watched feared he should faint and fall,
Yet durst not touch him.   For his wan lips prayed,
And his great heart, with each word syllabled,
Sped from its fount of love a fervent prayer.

But, presently, he bade them come and lift him,
And once more journeyed on with all his train.

Yet to another halting-place he drew;

THE APOSTLE OF THE ARDENNES

For, ere he died, he would make pilgrimage
Through the wide-reaching forest of Ardennes,
Marking as milestones all familiar spots,
Or clumps, or ancient trees, or rising knolls—
As one who, tossing through a sleepless night,
Must garner every half-forgotten deed
Of bygone days in his mind's granary,
To seal close with a sigh, or smile, or tear.

Here, amid densest leafy domes and aisles,
Uprose a chapel, small, yet goodly wrought
Of marble, carved to lacework dextrously
O'er the low door, as though sea-foam were laid,
Fresh from blue waves, to crest and garnish it;
Or, as if blossomful wild cherry trees,
A-bending from their stately height to kiss
The sacred walls they sheltered from rough winds,
Had dropt in snowy drift their purest petals
That presently grew cold and turned to stone.
In this same spot ten years had Hubert dwelt,

THE APOSTLE OF THE ARDENNES

An hermit, weaving robes of discipline
Upon the golden loom that Lantbert raised,
Or dreaming calmly from the bed of moss
His own hands stored within a wattled hut—
That hut the chrysalis of new-found life
That should be, as a chapel, vowed to God.
Thus, when probation years were passed and gone,
And he, Prince Hubert, held the Bishop's seat—
Bishop of Tongern and of Liège—accounted
Worthy to tread in holy Lantbert's steps,
Nay, more than worthy, and of great renown—
He bade the best, most skilled, of artisans
Build him a chapel, fair as holy thought,
With naught of common worth or make therein,
And white-winged, as uplift from earthly toil,
To spread perpetual pæans to the sky.

Lo! as he knelt upon yon narrow floor,
That was of porphyry and onyx rare
With sapphire lapis richly interlaid,

THE APOSTLE OF THE ARDENNES

And none beside him—not e'en Floribert—
Because he fain would seek his soul alone,
With it to bide in loneness as of old—
Amid the forest silence as of old—
And while warm sunlight streamed upon the apse,
Where gemmed mosaic gloriously portrayed
The Christ, high-seated, and, on either hand,
The apostles, twelve white sheep, who meekly stood
Watching His lifted finger for a sign—
It seemed to Hubert as there floated faint,
From out the greenwood, to his listening ear,
Strange drone of voices multitudinous,
Low echoing breaths that brought anear and shaped
An ancient lay, while memory's wand evoked
The vision of rough herdsmen, passing by,
Trolling their wild refrain : " Great father Pan—"
A struggling kid caught in their cruel grasp :
" O hearken, father Pan ! "

                                So had they hymned,

THE APOSTLE OF THE ARDENNES

Those untaught churls, in barbarous heathen times,
Calling the leering satyrs to their aid,
While, at the shrine of Dian, hunters bowed
To give the goddess share of woodland spoil.
Nay, yet a ghastlier sacrifice had oft,
With human blood, stained reeking red the ground,
For sake of idols wrought of stone or wood,
Before whose altars shrieked in hideous joy
The savage priests that on their own knives fell,
Drunk with full glut of ignorance and lust.
But, as he prayed—and down the furrowed cheeks
Of him, well named "Apostle of Ardennes,"
Salt tears of pity for this world of sin
Fell fast and free—nigh drew the chaunt, and nigher;
No pagan song, but surely, such a creed
As they hold dear who fight for Christian faith,
And fain would strike all heathen myths to earth.
Strong-armed for valorous deeds, to weak things kind,
Help of the helpless, comrades tried and leal,
Wearing beneath their robe of woven wool

THE APOSTLE OF THE ARDENNES

The breastplate of true courage, and on high
Lifting the sacred Rood—they drew anear,
Bronzed way-worn pilgrims, chaunting loud, the while
Their sandalled feet beat time in unison.

    "Soldier of Christ, arise!
       The dark night falls,
       The bugle calls!
And past these dusky woods and meres,
Beyond the hills, from silver spheres
That vibrate in the shadowy skies,
    Thy King, thy Master, calls.

    Himself has led the way
       O'er crumbling bridge
       And rocky ridge,
Himself with bleeding feet has tried
The fastness of the mountain side.
Fight on, ere comes the dawn of day—
    Thou too shalt win the ridge!

THE APOSTLE OF THE ARDENNES

  Soldier of Christ, stand fast.!
  Before thee looms the foe—
   Death's vale below—
Yet shrink not, fail not. Storm the height,
Let strength and might defend the right !
Behold victorious day at last,
   And at thy feet the foe ! "

Again the prelate and his train went forth.
Alas ! so weakly moved the aged chief,
Spent by keen pain and fever, that he scarce
(They deemed) might reach an earthly goal, or ere
The impatient spirit, parting from its coil,
Should rise in flight ; yet he with eagerness
Burned as a lamp that flares before it dies,
And "onward, onward," still his parched lips framed
That one persistent note, the battle-cry
Of all brave toilers.

     Homeward would he go.

THE APOSTLE OF THE ARDENNES

Nay, not to Liège, not to palatial halls,
Where he, the priest-king, still must servant be
Of countless vassals whom he called his flock,
And don the hair-shirt of an hundred duties
To chafe his weary soul 'spite failing strength.
Nay, not to Liège, but to a simpler realm—
An homestead that had once been Floriban's,
Where garden lilies still brought dreams of her,
And bending trees still whispered of her name,
Where milk-white swans slid noiseless down the mere,
And merle and mavis piped from fruited boughs.
There, only calm-browed monks paced in and out
Green alleys which her girlish rule made fair.
There should the press of state be well forgot,
And carking cares be driven out as thieves;
For comes not peace, with evening of our days,
Like twilight, when the heat and glare of sun
Drift from the sky ere advent of dark night?
Though to some natures, fierce as southern climes,
Such grey and temperate hours be all unknown.

THE APOSTLE OF THE ARDENNES

Yea, fain would he push on in search of peace.
So presently took boat, for surer progress,
Being too feeble now to sit his steed.

Soon, having laid him down for space of rest,
His heavy eyelids closed, and sleep o'ercame him.
Awhile he drowsed in calm unconscious trance,
While swiftly sped the boat, and all was hushed,
Save for the plash of oars, soft-struck as though,
Monotonous, the water-spirits drew
Deep breath in unison—while winds unfelt
Spread lazy circlings toward the drooping boughs
That, listless, motioned not.

                        O'er-taxed, in truth,
Was his worn strength, because so freely given,
With lavish gift, as from full purse and heart,
To all that prayed for succour in their need.
Thus, as he lay, it seemed that pallid Death
Played changeling to the warder Sleep, so watched

THE APOSTLE OF THE ARDENNES

'Stead him awhile o'er that imprisoned soul
Which at the wan lips scarce essayed to sigh,
Or through sunk eyelids quiver.   But the men
Who thronged the boat (Floribert not at hand)
Began to curse and wrangle, bandying taunts—
Their evil natures rising fierce and free.

Then dreamed the slumberer.

                        And behold! yon forest
Changed quick to grey-green hills, where olives
    climbed,
And vines spread o'er the stony steep, and down
Dry crevices the scarlet lilies flamed,
More glorious in their robes than Solomon;
While on the lake—Gennesareth's broad sea—
An open boat rocked, heaving first quite slowly,
Next in the wind's mouth but a toy, and last,
Tossed from the crested billows to deep troughs,
And lifted swift again, with strain and moan,

THE APOSTLE OF THE ARDENNES

While they who voyaged grew afraid, and strove
To stem the buffet of the storm, but could not;
So, vanquished, cried aloud, thinking to die.
But, in the hinder part of that frail vessel,
A figure clothed in white lay calm, and slept,
Nor heeded danger, nay, nor moil and wrack,
Nor was awoken by the whirlwind's roar,
But only last by voice of those around:
"Help, Lord, we perish!" Then he stirred, and bade
The wind be hushed, the sea obey, and peace,
For balm, drop softly on all troubled hearts.

Likewise, the dreaming Hubert woke to clamour,
And raging storm, and altercation fierce,
And brooding looks that menaced speedy flash
Of vengeful weapons, bringing hurt and blood.
So cried he: "Peace, be still," and yet again,
In speech divine for soothing of the storm,
(With wide-oped eyes alight through memory
Of that sweet dream of Christ,) called he aloud:

THE APOSTLE OF THE ARDENNES

"Peace, peace, be still!" Thus angry voices lulled,
And stubborn looks and hands were sudden quelled,
And, shamed, the waves of passion fell to calm.
To those around it seemed the White Christ rose,
From their own vessel's prow, rebuking them.
Silent they gazed.

            Yea, passion fell to calm.
No sound again, save plashing of slow oars,
Or overhead the cry of some wild bird
That, 'frighted, winged from forest shade to shade.

Soon after came they to the homestead path;
And once more was he placed upon his steed,
For faithful hands and strong must now uphold
In that familiar seat the form of one
Erst named Hubert the Hunter, king of men,
Who ne'er before for mortal help had craved.
Yet, as his servants bore him tenderly

THE APOSTLE OF THE ARDENNES

Along the grassy paths, his valiant spirit,
Which might not quail nor weakly be dismayed,
Made beautiful his face as with strange light,
Though racked he was by fever's ache and chill,
And by a cruel festering wound that long
Had maimed his hand.

                    Then, as he slowly rode,
Upheld thus in the saddle, and most faint,
The monastery of his choice loomed white
Before him, walls and cloisters shining clear,
And yet more ghostly blanched and purified
By the refulgence of the round white moon,
Which, like a saintly life in foul surrounding,
Made light more light, but darkness blacker yet.

Swift, with red torches, came the monks to meet
Their princely prelate, chaunting as they neared,
So knelt for blessing, yea, from first to last,
Abbot and youngest novice dwelling there;

THE APOSTLE OF THE ARDENNES

But heavy-hearted, through the pain of love.
All knew, alas! how he, their Saint of God,
Himself had told Death's fleet and sure approach,
Being in sleep divinely shown as vision
A new basilica, for him achieved,
Nor made by earthly hands.

       Fain would the abbot
Draw choicest wines, but Hubert said him nay.
Straight to the chapel must he hie, and there
Before the altar bend his faltering knees,
And kiss the altar horns, so place himself
Within the sanctuary of sanctuaries,
Lest his last hour come on him unaware.
Thus did he, and thereafter, fainting, spent,
Unto his couch right helpless was he borne;
And lay there, prostrate, conscious of no hurt,
Yet might not sleep for very weariness.
But through the night he to himself rehearsed—
A second David—supplicating Psalms

THE APOSTLE OF THE ARDENNES

Sung by the Hebrew man of God of yore,
Who, crying in his need, as Hubert cried,
Poured forth his soul in sorrow to the Lord.
Thus lived the saint three wakeful nights and days,
Though scarce in touch with life, for his sick mind,
Harassed by fever, went a-wandering forth
Amid the 'wildering maze of bygone times.

Awhile he deemed himself a child again,
Sporting with toys beside his mother's knee;
Or, at King Pepin's court, a noble youth,
Whose southern fire flowed hotly through his veins,
He'd teach the Belgic sluggards how to joust
Or spell the ballad-rhymes of Aquitaine.
Anon he turned his eyes, bedewed with tears,
To woo sweet Floriban, and bid her step
Down from her proud domain to grant her hand.
Next would he go a-hunting, and, embalmed,
As odorous roses in love-letters laid,
Breathed from his lips the old familiar call

THE APOSTLE OF THE ARDENNES

To horse or hound. Next, haply, Lantbert spake;
And with bent head his meek disciple heard,
And straight betook himself to forest depths,
With escort of the chorussing sweet birds.
Or, spirit-wise, he travelled back to Rome,
And viewed the sunset from the Pincian hill.
Power, as a robe, was o'er his shoulders spread;
He framed new laws, built cities, ruled the land—
The very land where he aforetime learned
The ruling of his own so haughty spirit;
Yea, as from out his heart had erst been torn
Fierce greed, and love of self, and lust of life,
Thence drave he all the gods of heathenesse.
Were these the words: "The Lord my shepherd is"?
Lo! through the darkness twelve white sheep of
    Christ
Wrought on blue apse, amid the forest vert,
Filed past in phantasy, while tinkled out
Most pastoral-wise a slender convent bell
That called the brethren to their nightly prayer:

THE APOSTLE OF THE ARDENNES

The Lord of hosts my tender Shepherd is—
Thus surely chimed yon echoing refrain.

But, as the aged prince yet dreamed and prayed,
The Tempter—that old enemy of man,
Who fain draws sword when man lies prone and weak
Through wound, or ill, or spirit weariness,
Nor is ashamed to don Death's ghostly cloak
And so to scare the feebly-beating heart—
He, Lucifer, that spied "God's champion" laid
On this last bed of sickness, sorely spent,
The worn soul well-nigh from the body riven,
The body well-nigh withered from the soul—
Drew nigh a-tiptoe, fearing now no longer,
But calling up all evil trolls and slaves
To conjure visions and evoke dread sights,
Thus with a thousand fears to assail the saint,
And with their poisoned arrows, sped from hell,
Probe deep, and with their black and bat-like wings
Veil the pure sky from his dim eyes o'er-strained,

THE APOSTLE OF THE ARDENNES

And, hideously grimacing, groan and curse,
Though but one hearing should admit the noise.

Then he that lay a-dying raised his voice,
'Ware of the presence of such combatant
As valiance of his right arm oft o'erthrew
In fairer days; and cried, entreating sore:

"Bring holy water blent with holy salt,
Yea, sprinkle all, and let sweet oil thrice blest
Be the defence of this my failing strength,
While silent prayers that pious brethren lift
Portend my drooping courage heavenward.
Chill is the dew—methinks the forest thickens,
Closing more dense about my tangled feet.
So low the branches sweep they strike mine eyes!"

But—on the fourth day—as the evening neared,
It seemed the burdened soul might cast aside
The trammels of an earthly frame opprest,
And, for a space, breathe free with life renewed.

THE APOSTLE OF THE ARDENNES

Then Floribert, obeying his behest,
Kneeling beside the well-belov'd, read low,
From out a volume small and velvet-bound,
Writ in the Latin tongue. And this the text:

"Our Lord, on Calvary's steep ascent,
Beneath His weighty cross sore bent,
With faintness faltered as He went.

A pious woman, dwelling near,
That saw Him fall—the Christ so dear—
With none beside to help or cheer,

While sweat and blood from thorny crown
His pallid face dropt fast adown,
Stript her white veil from off her gown,

And stanched the drops. Lo! when again
He trod the bitter path of pain,
His image on the cloth made stain.

THE APOSTLE OF THE ARDENNES

His lineaments of heavenly mould
Showed clear upon the linen's fold,
Unfading, though this world grow old:

His eyes divine, His wreath of shame,
His smile of grief, His hair of flame—
Veronica, the woman's name."

Then Hubert spake: "Yea, may God's likeness be
Imprinted, dear my son, on us, limned true;
That, in His image made, we show the world
His holy beauty wheresoe'er we go.
And ye, disciples—brethren—hearken now—
I fain would ride as herald to your courts.
Hear then my message; dwell in faith and hope,
And still in penitence, for Death comes soon.
Who spurns the crier nathless fears the Judge.
Nay, now I tremble—a poor sinner, I
That soon before my Judge must naked stand,
And of long stewardship give full account.
What should I say—unworthy as I am?

THE APOSTLE OF THE ARDENNES

But this one thing—behold, the souls I taught!
Here be my children who have learned Thy laws."

Next kept he silence, and yet presently :

" Have I not seen—within the sacred porch
Of our cathedral's wondrous carven gate—
That western gate, cold as a virgin's brow
Till bends the round sun, flushing with his kiss
To rosy radiance of a sudden joy—
Some little sparrow build her homely nest
Above the storied saints and great archangels,
Daring to dwell high o'er their outspread wings,
Close, close unto the image of our God?
So would I climb and fain would build and make
Mine habitation in the palm of Him
Who stretcheth out a saving hand to me,
Least worthy of His creatures.

. . . .

" Floribert!
On thee, perchance, devolve my earthly cares,

THE APOSTLE OF THE ARDENNES

With purse and cherished realm and bishopric,
So thou shouldst better all was done before.
The times are with thee—pagan creeds are dead ;
New light, new life, dawn for our prosperous land.
Methinks that my far-seeing spirit hails
The sunlight of such greatness as shall flood
Wide Gaul and Allemayne in future years
With richness, peace, and learning, and, for crown,
Brave piety to raise tall belfry towers
Pointing out prayer—an hundred where we've one—
Whose loud-voiced organs, from their golden throats
(As those which from the far east came of late)
Uplift all hearts. If thine the legacy,
Take thou my crook ; tend thou my well-loved flock,
So men shall say: his father but foreshadowed
Our noble Bishop in his stedfast path,
Who likens more the grace Divine of Him
That leads the herdsmen angels with the sheep.
Cease not to rule, yet ruling patient serve.
Spend thou great treasure, yet in doling be

THE APOSTLE OF THE ARDENNES

Thyself in need of dole, because so poor;
Most meek because supreme; for ancient birth
Taking the meanest seat among thy serfs.
Raise and arm fortresses, and build just laws,
Bind wounds, and succour eke the rich and poor;
Be loved by them, feared by thy country's foes;
Prince, knight and priest, be Purity thy shield.
And now farewell, for with this world I've done.
Pray for me, brethren, in my bitter need!
Howe'er environed by our lealest friends,
Alone we go when Death, on his pale horse,
Beckons the trembling soul toward dusky paths
Of yon chill moorland never trod before."

. . . . . .

Then they that saw God's holy champion swoon—
The heavy dews thick-beaded on his brow—
Knelt nigh about his bed, and kissed his feet,
With warm tears coursing down their cheeks as rain;
So dolorous they, by anguish sore o'erwhelmed.
But he, through Sacramental peace made glad,

THE APOSTLE OF THE ARDENNES

As if in dream yet strove to falter psalms;
Nor ceased—though weary hours, like lengthening shades,
Crept to the darkness of this last sad night,
And climbed steps tenebrous unto the dawn.
Nay, with the saffron streak of early day
His dauntless spirit flickered once again.
And Floribert he called:

                      "Spread thou thy cloak
To cover close my face—for now I die. . . .
The journey's end . . . still, still be Christ my guide."

Wherewith, 'mid sighs, he murmured forth the creed,
Banner of Faith he had so long upheld,
Firm clasp'd in death as such true knight beseemed.
Straightway thereon his glorious soul took flight,
And left our weeping world. There now lay prone
Naught but the earthly tenement of him
Who but a moment syne had gently sung
The praise of God, his Sender for our weal,
Or smiled in love on those that thronged anear.

THE APOSTLE OF THE ARDENNES

Yea, his great heart had ceased to beat for us.
The Christ, Who wrought that heart like to His own,
Would have it henceforth nigh His golden seat,
And, while men grieved because their saint had died,
Heaven's angels took a brother by the hand.

Thus did the holy Hubert pass away,
Though ne'er has passed his grace of fame and name.
Within the abbey he had built he lay,
And of great splendour were his obsequies.
But, while that priests and prelates mourned their prince,
And all the land lay dusked in pomp of gloom,
The poor, the sick, the widows, and the lame,
Blind men and lepers, ay, the outcast folk,
Wept for a father who had shared their woes.

Thus did the holy Hubert pass away.
And, with long ages, walls upraised by man,
As man himself, do drop and melt and end.
So falls the dark sarcophagus asunder,
And, phoenix-like, new domes and arches rise.

THE APOSTLE OF THE ARDENNES

Yea, sacred bones as precious relics lie
Where shrine and city may pronounce their name.
Yet woodmen in the twilight whisper low
How none may guess the certain resting-bed
Of him that was redeemer of his race.
For sure his body owns the green Ardennes
As wrapping shroud, above him hoary trees;
Their leafy boughs for burial canopy,
And velvet moss and snow-white bloom for pall;
While bluebells write his name each early spring,
And at his head the nodding aspen sighs,
And bracken creeps bedewed about his feet.
Yea, where at peace should saintly Hubert rest
Save that it be the core of green Ardennes?
For, when the furtive deer pass down the glade,
Perchance at some small rill to slake their thirst,
They pause, and, large-eyed, gaze with mournful look
As who should say: here sleeps that hermit mild
That was our friend. And flocks of tiny birds
Draw ofttimes near to chaunt his requiem,

THE APOSTLE OF THE ARDENNES

And through the blueness of a summer night,
With breast against a thorn, the nightingale
Sings of the birth of perfect life through pain.
So all the wild and forest things know well
That he—apostle of Ardennes—sleeps soft
In some cathedral cloister of the wood.

Thus did the holy Hubert pass away,
While through the centuries his name yet lives.
Still, still the staff he touched, the stole he wore,
The key he held, are blest and sacred things;
And haply, in that he had tamed the beasts,
And turned wild lust to peace and tender love,
And taught the pagan pride to kiss the cross,
And doffed his royal robes for pilgrim weeds,
His spirit, ay, his very name, yet tames
The wayward madness both of man and hound,
And brings all savage hearts to gentleness.

PRINTED BY
TURNBULL AND SPEARS,
EDINBURGH

By the Same Author

THE FLOWER SELLER

AND OTHER POEMS

PRESS OPINIONS

Daily News.—"A collection of pieces, finely felt and finely fashioned, from first to last."

Speaker.—"The thought has grown richer and deeper ; the style is surer, and, while not losing its simplicity, is often marked by an extreme dignity and beauty; and in many passages these poems arrive within the higher domains of poetry."

World.—"In the 'Flower Seller and other Poems' (Longmans), by Lady Lindsay, we have the best that she has yet given us. The refined thought and musical utterance of her former poems are here, but she strikes a higher note in 'Outremer,' and the sonnets of this volume are more finely finished. Very beautiful is the story of the waiting and the longing of the painter monk for that 'Promised shaft of blue.' 'The Flower Seller' is beautiful also ; not so subtle and heart-searching as 'Outremer,' but a fine strain of romance, full of colour, stateliness, and the mortal ill of a love as innocent as it is impossible."

Globe.—"Lady Lindsay again shows considerable command of varied metre, which she handles easily, but her best and most lasting work, perhaps, takes the sonnet form. Here, also, is the individuality of thought and feeling and expression—a pleasant freshness in the choice of subjects and the mode of dealing with them."

Glasgow Herald.—"Lady Lindsay's new book begins with a pleasing tale, admirably told."

Scotsman.—"A dainty elegance, shown in a sonnet sequence and in a cycle of songs like Tennyson's 'The Window,' both of which exhibit many felicities in the handling of difficult forms of verse."

Daily Telegraph.—"In her sonnets Lady Lindsay is seen to best advantage."

Birmingham Gazette.—"The volume . . . contains much that betokens that the accomplished writer has the artistic sense and poetic sense, with beauty and loftiness of thought and no mean power of expression."

Academy.—"This mystical legend ('Outremer') is set forth with delicacy and charm. But more charming still are some of Lady Lindsay's lyrics. . . . These not infrequently possess a free and spontaneous quality that reminds one of the bird that 'starts into song one moment—then is still.'"

Pall Mall Gazette.—"Lady Lindsay writes with a graceful and facile pen, and rhyme and rhythm are ready to her hand. There is much thought and pathos in her little volume. Perhaps the shorter lyrics show most poetical power, though 'In Sleep' and 'The Gentle Knight' are finely finished work, and 'West of the Mountains' is a tiny flawless gem."

Daily Courier.—"Lady Lindsay proves that her faculty for musical verse is as fresh and buoyant as ever. Meanwhile, in increasing the volume of her verse she has added to its strength; and the degree in which she has combined strength with sweetness is as rare as it is stimulating."

Morning Post.—"'The Flower Seller' which stands in the fore-front, is clearly inferior to most of the poems which follow it, and particularly to the charming and brightly-written piece which is second in order, and which graphically portrays the influences of art and religion on the romantic mind of a cloistered monk. Decidedly poetical, too, is 'Long years after,' with its pathetic thoughts of the past—and, in a very different style, 'The Stormy Petrel' is spirited and excellent."

Illustrated Sporting and Dramatic News.—"Lady Lindsay is so conscientious a worker, that it is scarcely surprising to find her rapidly coming into the front rank of poets."

Queen.—"It ('The Flower Seller') is distinctly the most striking poem I have read for a long time by anyone but our most recognised poets. Its charm, as I have said, is not in tricks of finish, but in the wealth of imagination and beauty with which the picture is presented to us."

THE KING'S LAST VIGIL

AND OTHER POEMS

THIRD EDITION

PRESS OPINIONS

Of "The King's Last Vigil" Mr Gladstone wrote: "It appears to me that the idea is very poetical; and the expression of it in a tone so reverent and tender cannot but do good."

Times.—"Lady Lindsay has generous sympathies, graceful fancy, skill and variety of versification, a wide reach of thought, and a broad range of theme.... Amongst contemporary singers, Lady Lindsay should take no undistinguished rank."

New Review.—"It may at least be maintained that she combines them" (the secrets of simplicity and distinction) "in a very high degree, in a degree not too common in contemporary art, and in a degree that proves her to be touched with the true inaccessible spirit of poetry, the spirit which (to use the outworn formula) is born and not created."

Speaker.—"This volume contains a notable deal of genuine poetry, expressed with admirable art."

World.—"The little touches of mirth, the sweet and solemn tones of melancholy, the bird music, and the fine correctness and completeness of the sonnet forms in which some of the best and highest thoughts of the poetess find expression, are equally rare and admirable."

Globe.—"Lady Lindsay's new book will increase and intensify her reputation as a writer of melodious and effective verse..... The general level of her workmanship is high—so high indeed that it is not easy to make selection of examples."

Glasgow Herald.—"The whole book is full of charm."

Star.—"I have long been an admirer of Lady Lindsay's children's poetry, but in this new volume, 'The King's Last Vigil, and other Poems,' she shows herself capable of work of more serious artistic significance and no less charm."

Sun.—"Lady Lindsay is one of the few among present-day poets who write verse that is simple, that expresses sentiment and emotion in restrained yet effective words; that is graceful without being namby-pamby, delicate without being finnicking. Her lines have melody, strength, and grace."

Scotsman.—"The versification is always faultless."

Observer.—"In the book of 'Lyrics' and the verses for children, entitled 'A String of Beads,' Lady Lindsay had shown the world that she possessed considerable literary faculty in addition to genuine poetic feeling, and the variety of her poetical attainments is still further exemplified in this new volume."

Illustrated London News.—"Her 'Lyrics,' belonging to the present decade, and, followed by 'A String of Beads' only two years ago, secure for her an honourable place in any future collection. And now comes a new volume, called 'The King's Last Vigil,' of more importance in size and in range of subject, if not in art and beauty, than either of its predecessors. . . . . A new, as well as a charmingly simple and sincere, note is struck by Lady Lindsay in her lines 'To My Own Face.' . . . For all this, and for much more that her volume gives us of answering charm, she holds the respects and admiration of her readers."

Irish Daily Independent.—"These poems are musical, sweet and tender, and reveal a beautiful nature."

Sunday Times.—"The whole book will be read with pleasure."

Birmingham Daily Post.—"The sweetness and sincerity of the graceful and simple poems is the abiding impression."

Liberal.—"In such pieces as 'Told in the Orchard,' 'A Violin Maker in the North,' 'Il mare mi chiama,' 'On the Morrow,' 'The Lover's Story,' she strikes a note distinctively original, like the song of some bird in the woodland, careless and free, singing for the sheer love of song. Many of her pieces, and these her best, are tremulous with a deep and profound pathos, evoked by the dread mystery of life and the vicarious suffering everywhere visible."

Queen.—"Lady Lindsay's new volume of verse shows a high level of attainment among the singers that are so numerous around us at the present day. . . . . We must strongly commend Lady Lindsay's latest volume to all lovers of poetry."

Academy.—"So much applause has been showered on this little book that it is not easy to speak temperately. . . . . Lady Lindsay is a poetess of real charm: it is easy to concede so much, but as yet she cannot claim exalted rank. . . . . She has in her the makings of a fine poet."

Nature Notes.—"No critic would be slow to acknowledge the many charms of this dainty little book."

Vanity Fair.—"Her poems are of the type that bear reading and re-reading."

Woman.—"I have come to the conclusion that Lady Lindsay is a real poet, but that she writes real poetry only now and then. Some of the things in the book linger in the memory by reason of their music, their true sentiment, and their fitting expression, and for these the volume is worth having."

Dublin Express.—"The proof of his" (Mr Gladstone's) "discernment is seen in the fact that a second edition of these poems has been called for in little more than a month since the issue of the first. . . . . In a time when England is once again 'a nest of singing birds,' Lady Lindsay is to be congratulated on possessing a note distinctly her own."

Dundee Advertiser.—"A book which in all it contains does honour to a singer of marked poetic gift."

Sketch.—"A good many readers may have a pleasant memory of Lady Lindsay's verses for children, 'A String of Beads.' In her new volume of poems, 'The King's Last Vigil,' she seeks a wider audience, and with considerable success. . . . There is something to be keenly grateful for in this volume of sane and simple verse."

Pall Mall Gazette.—"By the way—the subject being the poetry of women—how intensely one acknowledges a justified poem in another woman's work. This is Lady Lindsay's sonnet, 'To My Own Face.' What she says there is true, beautiful, as old as the race, and has never been said before."

Pall Mall Magazine.—"The 'Ode to Father Time' somehow recalls an early French poet in love with life; there is true phantasy in 'The Mad Mother's Lullaby,' and true pathos in 'A Poor Ghost,' and many an artless match of song—like the 'Bulfinch' triolet—beguiles the reader's journey. Two of the sonnets are really memorable—'Love or Fame,' and 'In Remembrance.'"

Court Journal.—"'The King's Last Vigil.' . . . This is the title of the opening poem, which is an extremely beautiful little piece of work, simple in style, but thoughtfully conceived, and expressed with much grace of diction."

New Age.—"The sonnet 'To My Own Face' is the most subtle poem in a book where all is pleasing."

www.ingramcontent.com/pod-product-compliance
Lightning Source LLC
Chambersburg PA
CBHW022119160426
43197CB00009B/1091